The Spiral
of
Existence in Growth
and the
Crown of Eternal Life

*

Traumear

Paperback ISBN 978-0-244-78575-8

*

www.traumear.com

*

The purpose of works like the present is to help those who
Wish to come into the light of day – who desire the realization
Of their highest hopes in spite of their worst fears and who
Will not rest until they have carved out a niche for themselves
In the 'kingdom of heaven on earth', from where they may serve
that same purpose, not fighting evil but doing good. However
The struggle with the modern dilemma cleanses and frees them.
Always the spirit of truth is willing to abide with them, even
As they are willing to abide in it, endlessly patient with change.

(from page 138)

*

The Spiral of
Existence in Growth
and the Crown of Eternal Life

Surely science, the knowledge for understanding,
Should persuade us of the benefits of 'being around',
Rather than forcing us – the poor student first
And later the professional – into arcane systems
With their private lingo and their secret formulas.

Take for example the science called biology,
A tree with a hundred branches, all of which
Yield different blooms, none of which bear fruit
Because finally each draws its bogus strength
From half-truths, not from perceived reality.

We hear the sympathetic voices of those
Who would 'save the earth'. Ah, but for whom?
Surely for those who have, to some end,
Learned how to exist, how to grow productively,
Rather than championing prolonged survival.

How shall we exist on the earth here and now?
Why bother in the first place, when so much depends
On pain and misery, which does seem calculated
To draw our attention elsewhere – but where?
Surely this question deserves some attention.

Let those who have a notion of what is implied
By existence in the light of day, here on earth,
Make their useful contribution as well as they might.
Let them learn that the purpose of evil is to sharpen
Our taste for what is good and our tools for doing it.

* * *

As for me, I have decided to search out the meaning
In terms of what I call 'existence in growth'.
Whatever I come up with will be useful for others.
I should perhaps explain how I manage to arrive
At the knowledge I present here to my fellow man
For the purpose of understanding existence in growth.

Primarily there is the knowledge of those in the past
Who saw fit to make the propagation of wisdom
Their main concern and to that end they have left us
Their works – philosophy, poetry and music.
I mention those three specifically, in that order,
For they are what I draw on, in this present work.

We grow up and absorb a cultural affinity
Which stimulates in the background. Education reveals
Similarity of the past with present surroundings.
We actively combine the past with our experience.
What we learn, as we struggle to survive, so as to live,
We draw on secondarily, to prove our comprehension.

Thirdly, and perhaps crucially in my own case,
I submit to the spirit of truth, which is essential
for that final amalgamation of what is worth knowing.
Wisdom, revealed to the cooperative soul,
is needful nowadays, when the sheer plurality
of interests cries out for the unifying principle.

I believe it to be wrong to separate perception
From active performance. Research and experiment
in truth will not succeed except as the necessarily
benign tribute to our community. In other words
our god will teach us what we pass on to others,
not what we withhold for our private delectation.

*

2

I would like to explore a particular secret
At this late date, as night draws in;
Meanwhile, within, the soul would speak
Of the principle lively in all that grows.

The way we say that something 'grows'
Allows many a meaning for speculation
And long before the poet would exercise reflection
He checks all haste and prepares for spirit.

So I too refuse to insist on prescription
And rely instead on convenient leisure
While gradually the level in the cup rises
Since knowledge is a product of human nature.

Consider the mysterious goal of the spiral.
What are the three elements it resists
As it draws itself up, inwardly urged to it;
At the same time outwardly well determined?

Look now closely, is force at work,
Or do you suspect that fear undermines
Gentle progress towards ultimate success?
Do you notice a cause or a sign of uncertainty?

This I put forward as the first element:
We sense it deeply in ourselves as 'gravity',
We resist it and consequently it gains meaning –
On its own it is nothing, so we call it an element..

*

3

Here I stop for a moment to focus on meaning.
We supply it ourselves when we feel distraught
And can only imagine that something must exist,
Because we are moved – and so we give it a name.

So much for gravity then, which ever motivates,
Leaving in its wake that basic search for direction,
Not yet for this or for that, merely perhaps for
What we might call apology for imagined inertia.

All that tangibly exists on the earth's surface
And comes into being for a time, before it changes
Into something else, is determined to heed the elements;
Such as gravity, which it is bound to resist.

And then, in case this still needs clarification,
Spontaneous resistance surfaces as a pointed search,
As it rises out of that accidental darkness
To which we ourselves might refer as dream.

*

4

It's only natural, we say, when we mean 'No wonder!'
And perhaps right now this may be one of those moments
When we might, if we were to open our sleepy eyes,
Come face to face with the secret of our existence.

What after all does it mean to exist, to be around,
When we might instead snooze in our own capacious
Doll-like, insensitive cocoon, utterly at the mercy
Of the dark forces that ignore or slay at will?

Not that we should be expected to know, to be aware,
Of the risks we incur, so totally out of order
And tied to necessities no one can readily describe,
For this is the state of organic inanition.

Horrible indeed to contemplate. How one arrives here
We can only guess, since all is negative, deplete,
As though the very will to exist lay exhausted
Like a rotting kernel, blank in its battered shell.

Indeed we might say that here lies death at its leisure,
If that were not too extreme an idea, too fraught
With the antique horrors and terrors that still captivate
Innocent imagination, at moments of grief due to loss.

So instead, in order to safeguard precious sanity,
We speak of creation's womb, where all is immobile
And idle, and of course untouched by order or plan;
So indistinct must remain this state, like zero.

*

5

This much then, to bring our thought to the boundary
Where the uncreated thing has no notion of itself,
Being, as it were, bereft of elemental challenge
And as yet undisturbed by spirit that saves and creates.

Alas, we refer to a thing. Do we know what a thing is?
Lest we suppose we find ourselves here in the presence
Of nature inchoate, merely waiting to be structured
Or to be formed by our grand and superior will –

Oh no, a thing is what we have done, in our ignorance
Or due to an evil heart, when we should have known better,
To some being, indeed to whatever being was given
Into our care, and we took no pains to accomplish it.

Therefore there's not a thing that solicits our affinity
That cannot be reinstated in the realm of being,
To which end the only suitable knowledge we need
Is this: that the genuine essence of being is humanity.

*

6

Even as a work itself cannot properly begin
Out of the blue but it draws to the creator's attention
Some thing that languishes, for the lack of loving attention,
In dire straits, neglected or outside the gate

Of the selfish city, so too does a human creator then
Himself desire to be recognized by his work
And for his work, so that, whatever still remains
Of 'thingness' within his nature, shall be verified.

And we who gain our full recognition from him
Who inspires our work to begin with, we need no further
Acknowledgment, such as praise or public applause,
Safe and cherished as we are, nourished by his love.

And at the same time, those who praise our work
For the sake of those who continue to labour in ignorance
Do themselves good, it figures to their advantage;
It aids and abets the ease with which they prosper.

We resist gravity even at this height of our being.
We judge envy, jealousy and resentment in others
In our pursuit of what we deem worthy of attention,
When we should practice humility, mercy and mildness.

Elsewhere gravity, this inconspicuous element,
And foremost of the three we mentioned at the beginning,
Is deemed by some to be a 'thing' that must be 'overcome'
So that they may enter space, independently of time.

Others still speak of sins and search in themselves
For antidotes, which they then know as moral virtues,
And these are turned into weapons against evil in others:
Oh tragic misunderstanding of the Christian West!

How do we make our impression on those around us;
This is what it comes down to, when this resistance
Is finally accepted as a summons to human being
And not turned into vengeful or morbid reaction.

So when we arrive at the apex of our existence
We do not settle down, as we might in some heaven
But we turn and offer our gains to those who need them,
Who struggle with things and are still unable to exist.

Them we encourage and we hold up to them the mirror
Not of their own dire needs, not of their impoverishment,
But of divine justice and its merciful blandishment,
That they may initiate the spiral of their existence.

* *

7

Teasing apart the strands of what we mean by growth,
By lively existence in the first place, we are now invited
To contemplate the second element that enters the fray,
Namely in competition for successful survival.

We boldly call it 'justice', and what we mean by this
Is revealed in the very urge we feel in our bones
To concentrate all our energies upon a single enterprise
And not to be sidetracked by wishful thinking or lust.

We come upon gravity as we resist the first element
And justice appeals to us as we resist the second.
We may put it like that, and yet we do well to remember:
Our resistance is what makes these elements elemental.

The resistance is automatic. This is why we always fail
In all our attempts to picture these initial processes.
However we do well freely to imagine what goes on
Once we have achieved the ability to imagine distinctly.

At this point we might do well to check what we mean
By distinct imagination, which never leads us astray,
As when we confuse the 'thing' that is our responsibility
With the 'being' worthy of our own creative testimony.

So for example we might come up with a theory
By which we seek to explain the physical alteration
Of all that exists – however we fail to interpret
The passage of time, which we imagine indistinctly.

*

8

Justice then, like gravity, commands our attention
From the day we are born. Then we see the light of day,
Which light we at once imagine, for we seek to preserve
The least increment of progress, justified in that light.

The concentric spiral of ample justification
For every step we take in a forward direction
Would seem to lead us astray only to the extent
That we fail to imagine it distinctly, instead picturing it.

Cultures and civilizations, along with their religions,
Are never done justifying themselves to the world,
Because the element, for which they might be thankful –
I mean the justice inherent in their organic being –

Is trampled underfoot due to materialist gain
And then, as a consequence, justice is reinvented
As an infinite spectacle, partly political, judicial,
Partly psychic, as the need to appear in the right.

* *

Of course we make excuses for how we are
And this, in a sense, is only to be expected.
On account of pressure from above we feel depressed
And fail to see the justice of our condition.

What would it take to make us return wisely
And not ungrateful to that truthful spring within,
From which we may, on each and every occasion
Of malfeasance, draw more than sufficient justification?

What can we say to those who struggle deplorably
Within sight of perfect happiness, (or so it seems to them)
Snared by their outraged conscience, now at the mercy
Of misled self, now due to unfortunate behaviour?

What does it mean to preach salvation to one who
Insists that his native rights have not been recognized,
When in truth we are the sole guardians of our rights,
Marred by our own intransigence and belligerence?

Injustice readily spirals out of control
When those whose elementary nature has died –
Indeed whose very soul has become a 'thing' –
Take it upon themselves to correct the world.

Ailment and then predicament – a man's nerves –
Are readily overruled by a mighty God's disciples
Who see in virtue nothing but their right
To fling the need for self-correction to the devil.

* *

10

Happily we may return to the spiral's source
Where justice – fit of self with eternal world –
Rests in peace, and we, who now understand this,
May stake our claim in peace, guided by antiquity.

There's much that makes the modern spirit cleave
To spectacles of future-incantation,
To mass-disturbance of an ordered world
That in itself contains no shred of justice –

And therefore we would make ourselves behold
Glad tidings that reminded ancient sages
Of what they knew they needed, which was now
Delivered and it focussed their attention

On inward kingship, justice in the blood,
And when these marvels finally caught their fancy
They tore their clothes and marched before the people
In regal celebration of true justice.

* *

11

Two elements, as we searched, we identified:
Justice and gravity. Both begin within us
As automatic, elemental resistance,
In unawareness of the modern spirit.

And this, of course, presents us with a problem,
Though only insofar we are modern
And to the degree that we rely on that spirit
To do our thinking and feeling for us –

Which, to be sure, is never recommended.
Hence our study here, which at this point
Allows us to define, in retrospection,
What we call the spiral of existence in growth.

What this image will principally achieve
Is some clarity for the contemporary spirit
As seen in counterpoise to modern spirit,
Upon which we no longer wish to rely.

Therefore we posit gravity and justice
As two of the three elementary resistances
Within that realm of our human nature
To which modern spirit has no access.

We ourselves, however, may enter in this present
Mode of discrete discernment, and we ignore
All indiscrete demands for materialist proof
As reactions to the truth, caused by anxiety.

*

12

The ímage of the spíral máinly týpifies
The prínciple of recúrrence at a néw lével:
The réturn of opportúnity, after dúe depárture
And incréased ténsion, fóllowed by rést.

Grówth is nót mechánical but láwful.
We knów, that by éach orgánic béing –
And thís, of cóurse, inclúdes húman beings –
A cértain páttern is démonstráted.

We may gáin íntimate ínsight into ówn
Cháracter and personálity; bóth of thése
Shápe that páttern, and só we may táke
An ínterest in the grówth of óther béings.

Whatéver trúly exísts thérefore
Móves and ís moved ídiomátically,
While béings in commúnity desígn their ówn
Specífic 'spíral' to whích they adhére.

* *

The two main poles of existence on earth
We may justly name individuality and community.
We take care of ourselves for the sake of others
and this we may call the direction of the spiral.

It stands to reason that we as human beings
Have greater insight into human community
Than into the community of animals or plants
But all the same, those communities exist.

In other words, the individual plant exists
In that it takes care of itself so that it might
Take care of its particular plant community,
Which principle motivates all beings on earth.

So our primary purpose will always reside
In our ridding ourselves of all thing-knowledge
So that we may appreciate beings as they are,
Not forced or ignored due to modern criticism.

While we still adhere to the outdated notion
That human nature as such is flawed
And therefore separate from ideal nature
To which we look up as to some ideal god,

We cannot arrive, freely and magnanimously,
At knowledge and wisdom that suits our purpose,
As beings endowed with divine humanity
And therefore responsible for all earthly beings.

*

14

The modern mindset refuses to allow for
Humanity as the essence of being,
Hence the initial duality of soul
And the finality of the modern world system.

The modern earth cannot support
Created life because creation implies
The interconnectedness of all that exists
While modernity produces discrete individuals.

If we wish to grow on earth as beings
We must lay aside our humanist arrogance
And refuse to be swayed by human sacrifice:
The sacrifice of our soul to the flesh.

But how can we do this, since we know nothing else
Except matter and the psyche, both disoriented,
Both troublesome to the good intention
And more so to the genuinely good deed?

*

15

We may know that our very existence implies
An initial resistance of justice and gravity.
Right from the start these elements subsist
Within us, however in negative fashion.

The third element we have not yet named,
But these two cause what I propose to call
A negative potency within us, and this we may
Know or regret, either see or resent.

Much depends on how we choose,
On whether we choose or end up being swayed
By regret and resentment. This, then, is not
Specifically a matter for adult education.

Even the youngest child will be affected
By adults who either behave parentally
Or else they demonstrate regret and resentment
In the child's presence and directly to the child.

The dedicated adult learns and practices
What it means to set the parental example.
The onset of regret and resentment is recognized
As genuine incentive to renewal and understanding.

Sense and sensibility both result
From a caring attitude to material resistance.
It must seem to go against the grain to be stimulated
And then not to indulge the matter of the stimulus.

*

16

Creatively we identify these primary incentives
As such and then we behave in accordance.
Blessed are those who regret and then rejoice.
Blessed are those who resent and then respond.

Regret and *resentment* I employ as key concepts,
I hope that is understood. Regret, as we know,
May make us wish we had not been born
while resentment makes us wish the other were dead.

So murder and suicide proceed in a straight line
From what we may 'see', at its earliest occurrence,
Before we act creatively. I speak here to those
Who embrace their resurrection instead of escaping,

And not to those for whom the spiral of existence
Still has no meaning. They exist blindly.
This does not cause them the least trepidation,
Since god gives the gift of life as he chooses.

*

17

The time has come to search for the third element
That translates for us, along with gravity and justice,
The evidence we have, in our private and public life,
Of a repeated binding and loosing, and also of a

Constant prodding and prompting against our image,
Our identity, our self, as though the great danger were
Indifference, lack of interest, a case of standing still
In the face of what we customarily mean by our life.

Here again, we come up, initially, against an
Unmistakable negativity which we might feel
Persuaded, by the dictates of self-preservation,
To ignore if we can, or if we cannot, to dispute

Its original existence. I mean the element 'sun'.
We come, here, upon that old bugbear: electricity
And magnetism, which is never to be understood.
We may think of it as election and magnification.

The effect on us is on our nerves, on our brain.
Chaos describes it. We feel outclassed, outnumbered.
We tend to rush off to join a group of the like-minded,
In the hope that stability and balance will return to us.

Sun rises, sun sets and then there is high noon
When nothing much moves, our slovenly personality
Rises to the surface, we have some trouble identifying
The place where we started or where we are now.

*

18

Consequently, if we have our wits about us,
We may say to ourselves: Rub the sleep from your eyes;
Sluggard, make a move, and do it cheerfully, so that
Right away the blood begins to course through your veins.

In other words, sluggishness informs us that it's time
To liven things up. Apathy recommends itself
As the sign of the immediate presence in our nature
Of compassion and human-natural affection.

Please keep in mind, dear reader, that in terms of
These three elements we stand exposed
To the root of existence in growth – and that we make
For our benefit an imaginative and thoughtful doctrine.

Certainly there will be those who find this complicated
But let them be reminded that the study of fundamentals
Is to link up our nature, in places where it has separated,
With the nature of all beings, not only human beings.

*

19

Science is knowledge for the purpose of understanding,
So we may as well try to understand what it means
To exist rather than not to exist,
Especially while at liberty to refrain from existence.

It is the inborn right of all human beings
To set their will against their existence,
So that, instead of developing and evolving,
They survive until actual death takes them.

Existence, for them, means material expansion
And extension in time and space. In other words
They do not grow. No one can persuade them.
The die is cast for them. Their senses remain closed.

If we were all-knowing we would probably realize
That they too have a role to play
In the grand design of human evolution;
While we tolerate, we need not imitate or admire.

In comparison, some are to exist in growth
And do well to come to terms with those initial moves
In themselves that oppose existence, and to realize
That existence is not accident but creative choice.

What happens, therefore, at the start, is that we
Experience not so much an urgency to exist
But rather a more or less uncomfortable reminder
To cease from accidental pseudo-existence.

*

20

Also keep in mind that in our present employment
No attempt is made to exemplify what amounts to
'The whole human being', an ideal at best and
In any case more of a mythological achievement.

No, we have wisely decided to limit ourselves,
For the present time, at least, to that moment in history
When the cool appreciation of life lies uppermost
And the study of communication is left for another time.

I believe we have barely yet begun to acknowledge
How much our happiness and our simple pleasure
Depend on our ability to envision separately
Being in world and existence in growth.

Secretly we wonder whom we may thank
For this decided achievement, this remarkable feat
As it has come down to us during two millennia
So that even today we may make ends meet.

*

We return to sun now, the element we oppose
Decidedly to our detriment if we continue to oppose it.
How, we should ask now, does sun, in the particular,
Seem to cause in our nature this unfortunate antipathy.

However I dare say, what we might ask first,
In line with our earnest commitment as researchers, is:
How can it help us to know more about these elements
Than indeed their names, and to what end these?

To me it seems that these elements, as we named them –
Specifically gravity, justice and sun –
Carry a unique weight of experience
That touches each one of us in a slightly different way.

The effect is mythic – and the advantage of myth
Is throughout our life its organic spirituality,
which on one hand cautions us against hectic machinery
and on the other it lubricates the grinding intellect.

We may take the mythic influence for granted
But more than that, why not rely on these benefits
The way we rely on poetry and music
To ease us back into gentle humanity –

When once more the immediate exigencies of the day
Have unnerved us outside, beyond our comfort zone,
Where next we may hope to establish a foothold
In line with the enlivening demands of our growth.

*

22

So gravity directly relates us to the earth
And our aim, after all, is to exist on the earth,
So surely, would we not want to know in detail
If we were somehow guilty of opposing it?

The same, of course, goes for justice and sun.
Our particular being yearns for its original
Universal setting, while the enlivening influence
Of the sun would find us both ready and responsive.

Now while we think of our existence as merely
A case of 'being around' rather than absent,
We are bound to inherit, throughout many generations,
A massive backlog of growth-related data.

These data then soon mislead us into imagining
Our own human-natural gifts and talents
As circumscribed by countless tragic eventualities.
For centuries we are modern when we might be real.

*

23

Once again then, by accidentally opposing
These resistant affinities in our human nature –
These elemental increments that touch on all creation –
We set out on a course both obscure and problematic.

How this opposition works itself out
In every individual, society and nation,
Varies impressively and we become enamoured
By interest and by the will to unify and combine.

Alas, we have set out on a course of action
That remains unrooted while we persevere;
The loftiest notions fall short of fruition
And the respite we crave slips from our grasp.

Now and again a wise man appears
Who reminds us of what we have left unsourced.
Our most frequent response is really a reaction:
We hate to be reminded of our essential neglect.

And so, what we mean by our modern culture
And by civilization, is a record of our flight
from the dire consequences of an accidental opposition
to what would guarantee a most splendid success.

How can we bear to stand by idly
Once the truth within us has enlightened us!
How can we bear then that our brothers and sisters
Should not be informed of that elementary benefit!

*

24

"World environment is elemental. Its unavoidable
influx highlights or pinpoints those areas
in ourselves where more foundation is needed –
to support more life." This is a quotation from a

Book called: Nerve Energy and Psychic Phenomena.
It's available on the computer, the author is Traumear.
The same issue is scrutinized from another point of view.
How can we take advantage of the good we have resisted.

Until now, in this present book, we have only concentrated
On the nature of our resistance to present elements.
The effects of that resistance are, or course, accessible
Within us, in that realm to which we alone have entry.

It makes sense to think of those effects as elementary,
However the elements themselves, which we resist,
Make up the world-environment we experience
And this is a teaching we do well to take on board.

*

Once more the spiral takes a loftier turn
And oh, without warning, we find ourselves challenged
On two fronts – both lie within our capacity
And we turn to them now; first to one, then to the other.

Our world environment, insofar as we experience it,
Is composed of elements, infinite in number.
What shall we say of our world environment?
It is that it is – let there be no dishonesty.

Are we human beings, that we trade our integrity
For making a splash on the popular scene,
Or shall we perform as our god has created us,
Taking advantage of inherited genes?

All we have borne in our heart through the ages
Here it brings truth to its birthday at last.
Father, we no longer speak of irreverence
When the world reaches through our mortality.

Certainly this is not the world our schoolmasters
Drew on the blackboard to tire us out
But wonder upon wonder, now that we confess
Arrogant distortion, morbid cowardice.

The main thing here is that we know our limitation.
All too soon we project our weaknesses
Into what all surrounds us, man or beast,
The earth in general, the myth of a cosmogony.

*

26

Here in the meantime, growing within us
The foretold kingdom has come to fruition.
Up to us now to accommodate ourselves,
To begin the work that is based on humanity.

It does seem that we chose twilight zones
when in the past we staged our compositions.
What all we think and feel in the 'light of day'
Suits us just fine now, why should we complain?

Let's face it, we're far too busy checking out
The all too numerous errors of our past,
When we accepted what seemed wrong was wrong
And never once it struck us we were lying.

All is forgiven, this is true, but friends,
Consider, you may not yet have begun to live!
Waiting for you in secret is such a life that
Unless you make preparation it may well kill you.

* *

27

So let us for a moment take a closer look at what we mean
By our world environment, in which we live and to which
We look, as creative beings, for our personal experience.

And let us for a moment lay to one side what we mean
By such things as nature, politics, the society of our equals,
And also what we love, brothers and sisters in community.

Even in the time prior to our present era
There were also those who wished to construct a paradigm
Of all that exists, so that they might freely relate to it.

Usually gods were involved and sometimes morality;
The cause of motion, the underlying trends that would somehow
Explain what was happening, so that it might be predicted.

This is understandable, for nothing so much presses us
As blind fate, another word for our ignorance of the future,
And out of pain and bafflement one searches for truth.

At last, the gaze, fixed as it was for centuries
On the structures of the physical world, now turns inward
So that thought itself is questioned, both mortal and divine.

The thinking man takes pride in what he has created,
Compares it with what those before him, have achieved,
And man in his cosmos becomes progressively secure.

The gods, rather than regulating the affairs of man
Show him what tools he possesses so that he may arrive
At intelligent conclusions, with insight into law and order.

But mortals and immortals cannot share the same boon.
No one can say why some are gifted from birth
While others remain in a state of blind confusion.

'I inquire into myself' said the great Heraclitus
And opened the door to the diverse mysteries within.
Heroically he battled with the implications of his human frailty.

Thereafter the world held its breath. Knowledge diversified,
The sheer plurality of things and laws choked the system.
Impossible for mortal man to take that last step.

*

28

Darkness descended upon the earth. A mysterious despair
Coloured the bodies and souls of beings of every rank:
Someone – who knows where – will surely relieve us.

Out of the clouds? No. Out of the earth? Not at all, dear.
So long we have waited! Friendless, outside the gate.
All our knowledge, our energy, all exhausted.

When will the hero arrive? The great one. The one whose
Patience with us will be endless, whose comfort unstinting.
Surely the world in its languor has suffered enough!

Then he does come – not what we expected.
Dear me, not a warrior type at all.
More like someone who has lost his bearings.

But his words unhinge conventional meaning,
Interfere with what we know and cherish,
Lift us swiftly out of ancient ways.

And then he leaves. Our dream is shattered.
What we know as death removes his shape
From our sight and we are left with longing.

For several days we grope in the darkness,
Unable to join up promises with reality,
Sadly still equipped with our old language.

*

29

Then the sudden confusion of the senses,
Nothing any longer means what it seems.
Light within and without – it dances,
Even our wise ones see visions and dreams.

When the dust had settled, we looked at each other;
Not right away did we realize what had happened.
Most who had hoped found their hope was extended,
Some held their being completed in hand.

And ever since then, until this very day,
The world is full of dire misunderstanding,
Because nothing is more difficult, more problematic,
Than allowing our old self to be cast away.

*

30

The spiral takes another lofty turn.
Two-thousand years have drifted over the horizon.
Would you agree, dear friend, the time has come
Once more to face the flurry of the elements,
And this time not to choose but to be chosen?

Our world environment, elemental throughout,
Casts all other environments in the shadow.
Look, you can make your own mind up yourself,
Especially if you choose to limit your own actions,
Knowing that what affects you works to your advantage.

*

31

The spiral, where we do not wish to go,
Because we have resisted all along
The immediate influence of our world environment,
Would entertain us now, against our will,
By showing us what monsters we have become.

We choose to stay, for in our narrow minds
The love we have resisted has deposited
A token of itself, for us to inherit,
So that we might, at last, when the time is ripe,
Devote ourselves to mercy and to love.

Now gravity would plant our feet on earth
And so affect our flesh, our heart, our brain,
That finally the music of the spheres
Informs us of our own nobility,
Our sovereignty as loving human beings.

Now justice takes the reigns in her own hands
And we are led, so that we may know freedom
Within the endless concourse of all beings,

No longer interrupted by bad dreams
But knowing that what befalls us means our blessing.

Now sun, the final element we chose
So that this work might come into existence,
Cannot but cast its light upon a moon
That we might be accompanied through life
By one who mingles with our being her own.

All this succeeds because we have accepted
That single element that we did not choose
But it chose us, being love and merciful,
Against which nothing evil can hold out
But it must serve our powerful human being.

*

32

The essence of the spiral is that it returns on itself
Again and again, but always at a higher level.
Now and again we look back and say: I have been here
Before but now I know better and more, I have greater
Insight and powers of perception and I see further.

After the resurrection we are like unto the angels,
But here and now our glory as human beings
Shines on the firmament and announces itself within
With increasing beauty. We have our work cut out for us
As we expand the limits of the 'kingdom of god'.

Shall we not now, in our works, for those who have arrived
In the light, offer shade that will make the light less blinding?
Shall we not gently interfere with those who insist
That nothing can be done, since they will never be worthy?
Out of our endless supply we contribute appropriately.

Always there have been those who considered, in their fervour,
That the god who is love is willing to advance systematically
And so they come up with their orders, their secret societies,
With the best of intentions, but coercion carries the day
And spoils the well-laid plans of impatient intellects.

This is our mortality, that we experience the world
So that we accumulate matter with which we may build.
Alas this matter, as I have shown all along,
Lends itself readily to further material resistance,
Resistance not accidental now, but intentional.

In other words, now we are responsible for choosing the path
Of insolence, yes, and of downright psychic behaviour
Because we play along with the resistant character of matter
And nothing is achieved, but that first level of intransigence
Involves us in guilt and erects partitions between us.

Now we understand perfectly the genesis of materialism.
Oddly it turns out that the materialist knows nothing of matter.
Merely by resisting resistance he turns into a psychopath.
Or if that is too strong a word for him let him reflect
That his human-natural integrity has now been compromised.

On first reflection, when we realize we have resisted
The innocent world, what is the pang we feel
That seems to be part and parcel of our bare experience,
When we cannot shake off that sense of having broken something?
Do we not feel that in our innocence we have spoiled innocence?

Here, in our work, we have placed our finger on the spot
That indicates disturbingly the genesis of the modern spirit.
What we have done, and how we feel, that is given.
Neither for the one nor for the other can we be blamed,
So let us not speak of sin here, or of retribution.

Our initial existential step has left us in a quandary.
We have always loved the truth, but now it has landed us
In a most peculiar situation, where on one hand we feel
The need for justification, while on the other hand
We cannot think ill of ourselves for having done wrong.

* *

33

There are two ways now in which we can turn out modern.
Self-justification is the one, the other is morbidity.
We can say, quite correctly, that we have done nothing wrong.
After all we have experienced the world, that is human-natural.
And therefore that feeling of guilt needs to be expunged.

This is the one way, and from now on, along this path
We are bound to experience the world in the same old manner
And both our action and passion will be dogged with guilt
And also with shame, for which we have no explanation,
So we harden our hearts and continue on this path regardless.

Gravity draws us down and needs to be resisted.
The sun pulls us heavenward, which causes us anxiety
And justice continues to accuse us of what makes no sense to us.
Sadly the spiral of existence in growth is stuck.
Is it any wonder that we come down with cancer?

This illness is not existence *in* growth but *of* growth.
It demonstrates that growth is a necessary aspect of our being
And that it is we ourselves who need to grow,
Otherwise tumours end up doing the growing for us
And is it not as if we had our noses rubbed in their existence?

Increasingly we depend on appearances to justify our actions.
Whatever we do, we fear it might not be quite right,
So we sacrifice, we self-harm, in the hope that this will appease
Those accusative ghosts, that appear to look over our shoulder
As soon as we relax, hoping for some comfort, some rest.

Another one of our modern methods for assuaging
the accumulating inner insecurity is overproduction
on the basis of magical memes that hitch up the trousers
of those who support the burgeoning entertainment industry
with the notion that life is glitz, a Technicolor film.

Magic is the only high-class acceptable method
For making it look as if we had nothing to fear,
For look, after all, are we not in the pay of the devil
And who can blame us for finally feeling perfect,
Linking arms in a crowd of the like-minded?

What is the end of modernity along this one path
While the soul gradually trickles out onto the ground
And human being, in the end, becomes but a by-word
For latter-day inattention to social community,
So that our nervous ticks may rebuild the nation?

The question contains the answer. We are not to worry.
Everything is bound to come out alright in the end.
Only take care that those who have something to say
Out of the ordinary and perhaps linked to the truth
Are post-haste ridiculed and banned from the public screen.

The screen identifies the crunch of the post-modern left.
(Consider we have not yet touched on the post-modern right.)
Whatever behaves on the screen is cool, is acceptable
Because it makes no demands on our brain as a whole.
The medium overrules the most inconclusive message.

Syndromes proliferate: complex excuses for thoughtlessness.
Structures in the mind where lies can be stored and
maintained.
Health as ideal and old age as the goal of existence.
Art as the outlet for whatever just tickles your fancy.
Anything goes in public if it makes the front page.

'Eyes to the right' then, for spurious self-justification –
At times the political process can barely keep up
With all the demands for morals combined with legality,
In short, for rights for everything under the sun:
The right not to exist, to stop growing.

*

34

'Nose to the left' now, we return to look at the other path
That allows us to avoid reflection as we turn out modern.
The one was justification, the other – morbidity.
While we are morbid we bathe in that sense of guilt
Even though we know that no one has a right to blame us.

Alas, we cannot get away from the fact we feel blame.
We opened our eyes to the world – Oh dear! I'm sorry!
I apologize for being around. I'm a blot on the landscape.
I admit I shouldn't have opened my eyes in the first place.
Now that the damage is done, let me make restitution.

There must be an institution that will service my conscience,
My social conscience, the feeling that I have sinned,
Which is based on the fact that I feel that I have sinned
And god-given reason really has nothing to do with it.
I certainly enjoy that pleasure of self-mortification.

The institution I require to shore up my conscience,
Which requires ongoing confession and repeated sinning,
Shall be called a religion, which implies once again a congregation
Of the like-minded. That's important. When I'm alone
All too often it occurs to me that I might be responsible –

And then these disturbing thoughts crowd into my soul.
This, mind you, is liable to remind me I have a soul
But look, I'm addicted to the cow-warmth of mutual apology
For the error of being around, for the arrogance of growth,
So please support me, I promise to preach your dogma.

Let's face it, the Jesus who has bled for my self will do nicely.
With him in mind, we may settle down in our groove
Of antediluvian, high-minded post-modern consciousness –
Though still conveniently connected to the modern tradition
Of the past two millennia. – Let no one accuse me of apostasy.

Also, let's face it, Christianity is not the only religion.
A hundred others will offer similar comfort
To allow me to sustain indefinitely my shaky connection
With the world of beings, of human beings and otherwise;
A bond that is based entirely on what I dislike.

Of course I might base my existence on psychic phenomena,
On psychosomatic and psychomental hindrances
To my slovenly progress in the supernatural realm,
Where phobias, allergies, addictions roost like chickens
On my sorry insistence on self-identification.

This self-identification is a post-modern branch
Of the tree rooted in morbid self-appreciation.
I carefully refrain from asking who I might be,
In case, for once, I might enlist my brain as a whole,
And I ask instead, critically: Who might you be?

With a bit of luck this leads to endless discussion,
To opinion roasted on the charcoal of self-righteousness,
Until we fall out, and then there's plenty of time
For accusations of –isms: race, sex, national –
All of which helps me to avoid reflection on myself.

*

35

Now let's consider what we might do instead.
Would we perhaps do well to look at the beginning?
Here we have feasted our eyes on the tree of knowledge
And what we come down with is a bit like a bad cold.
The spirit moves but the flesh is dead as a doornail.

Certainly guilt and shame enter the precincts
Of the innocent mind, also of the body at ease.
For a moment we contemplate how we might respond
To what has suddenly drifted into our awareness,
And with this we take our time, as though time were endless.

Far from our mind are self-justification and morbidity
Because we are accustomed to be patient, even with our soul.
Nothing else happens. We wonder, do we exist?
Blessed gravity inspires us with a model foundation.
In this we resemble every other being on earth.

At this precise moment we realize we exist for a reason.
Oh such a tiny spark of knowledge has entered us.
We close our eyes and occupy the centre of our being
Gladly, because we sense a cheerful welcome
Where nothing else can enter nor be seen.

This is how we define our human being,
Ourselves earth-centred, extant at the centre of the universe.
Strange, how here we are neither at a loss nor superfluous.
Wonderful! Marvellous, how we can practically taste
The peace that shines within us at this time!

Too well brought up are we to wish to cling to it.
As a result nothing diminishes our gratitude
And oh the joy that leaves our spirit free
To reach once more into that endless world
And find ourselves enlivened and rewarded.

Happy the one who turns now to his friend
And shares with him the fullness of experience.
Oh most essential, human-natural deed!
We have discovered faith within our being;
The new beginning to entirely reborne life.

*

Then there are those who have missed their calling,
Who have felt the resistance within them and said:
This will drag me down but I'm made of sterner stuff,
No one shall tell me what to do. I'm a man
Who knows his mind and kowtows to no one.

Time after time there appears in his constitution
A veritable weakness, he senses it, but he mistakes
Its character and hates the depleting feel of it.
He heeds the voice of Society: Ignore!
Pretend that there is no inner weakness.

What he builds up then could be described as a fort
Around pretensions, downright lies and prejudices.
He is praised for every effort he makes
In that direction and joins the ranks of those
Who hate the truth and go to church to kill it.

Perhaps he calls himself a devout Christian.
The label identifies, confers distinction.
Or he becomes an atheist and looks down
On all religion from a lofty height.
Meanwhile, within him, the Christ bides his time.

*

It seems there's much that God can do, but much
God cannot do, for it depends on us.
Perhaps we've grown up within shouting distance
Of an Almighty God who rules the roost
And tumbles our best efforts at his will.

Close contact with a child of nature now,
Of human nature, works a double change
Within the one whose heart is not yet stone,
And he becomes confused, he struggles on –
He fears for his composure – for his sanity.

What all he has been taught, at school, at home,
Domestic cautions, humanist morality,
One night it all gives way, before a storm
Of psychic violence, so intense, so brutal
That what remains is but a whimpering child.

*

38

This too is one way, that we await the catastrophe,
When all that has been stacked on ritual shelves
Inside a morbid soul – while we took time
Once more to entertain the sexual passions –
Crumbles like dust and leaves us without hope:

Except that now we have the hope we craved.
Oh dear, I'd love to explain just what I mean
By hope now, which is nothing like the hope
For this and that. We cannot point it out
To one another, and there's no alternative.

This hope demands quite simply that we leave
Ourselves wide open for whatever moves
Towards us from the world in which we live
Because we understand that our god's grace
Arrives from world in which he keeps his peace –

Hope that is undermined by one thing only,
And I confess my reluctance even to name it.
It casts in doubt the very possibility
Of truth in person, here on earth, among us.
It sows contention in our hearts and minds.

We take a closer look at what we mean
By criticism if we choose to reflect
On our commitment to enhance the life
Of those who struggle within sight of truth
But yet they lack the courage to embrace it.

Most telling of their pain and characteristic
Of how they try to make the two ends meet –
The two ends of our spirit and our nature –
And we can see how close they come to step
Into the breach themselves – then arrives criticism,

The scourge of truth, and merrily informs them,
Perhaps by means of jest, by way of anecdote
Or sidelong glance to indicate superiority:
"You cause yourself unnecessary grief.
Do but accept your evil in good grace –

And look around; the world is half and half
And so must you be if you hope to thrive
And if our expectations to succeed
Are not curtailed by vain idolatry,
Such as this personality of the truth.

What is the truth, except twice two makes four,
And when you split some particle of resistance
Again in two, why, there's majestic proof
Of infinite division. Right is real,
Seek happiness, cling to health, the world's a spoof."

How, in the sickly light of such philosophy,
Can anyone who trembles on the brink
Of self-delusion find his way to a certainty
That does not in itself contain the germ
Of inward dissolution and outward destruction?

For two millennia have we serviced this spirit
Of criticism in one way or another,
Have made a point of 'rendering harmless' those
Whose voices showed some sign of true belief
By finding them 'a home' in some institution.

The modern gift is double-tongued, is fretful
of being prematurely cast in shade.
Science, religion, art – all fashion-fodder.
One hesitates to call it by the name
It gives itself and instead calls it progress.

Science, religion, art – if not modern
Make it their first task to avoid the criticism
That makes the wise man turn aside and smile.
Only a fool would rail against modernity.
Instead we make our contemporary moves.

* * *

39

At every beginning, where philosophy seeks to establish
A modus vivendi, not merely an intellectual system,
The Janus character of language is not only unavoidable
But truthfully functional, in the sense of 'before and after' –
First the old is unravelled and then comes the new.

For one example I quote from the Gospel of John:
'In a while you will not see me and then in a while
You will see me, because I go to the father.'
Imagine if he had said: 'You will see me again,'
As if the seeing before were the same as after!

Of course he might have explained: 'After I'm gone
You will have different eyes, your seeing will be different.'
Would that have prevented the two millennia of uncertainty
For those who neither accepted the man nor the message?
We see him now though we might not have seen him then.

I mention this to appease those whose intellect
Has not yet reflected upon its innate limitations.
Merciful spirit offers them apparent contradictions.
It encourages them thereby to die to the past,
The modern past, which cannot become contemporary.

So let this serve to explain why now and again
A word is Janus-faced, modern and contemporary.
If new life were suddenly presented in stark reality,
This would frighten off many, who are only confused
Because they have only ever experienced the past –

But the past is extinct if not open to the here and now.
Never let us presume that we know the future
Unless by the present past we imply extinction.
Never let us forget that in the here and now
We see the living past as our own future.

*

40

How do we grow out of resentment?
There must be a way that allows us to reverse
The sickening, cheap satisfaction with the status
Quo, hoping it will hold another while.

Freakish responses to perfectly normal
Suggestions trigger a rage that might at least
Appear sound under the surface. One elects to
Wait, and wait again, to buy time.

I suspect I may not be entirely clued in
With respect to time. Oh I respect it, but
Now and again it curls up in a corner and
Twitches like a cat with bad nerves.

Would that be the time then for a radical
Interference with the status quo, or should I
Leaf through a book of poems in case
A bit of black print speaks clearly?

Resentment has ensconced itself so thoroughly
Within my within-parts (I can't imagine closer)
That I have to act. This, presently, is me
Acting, from the core of my best intention.

Growth, you see, is not something a person can
Picture. It's a hound's tooth suddenly broken
Off in a carcase, where the backbone split
When one had a perfect right to satisfaction.

Not that we find ourselves always again at the
Beginning but I would remind you of that,
So we cross-check, bring measurement to bear,
Cough loudly, then thread the needle again.

Above all else don't measure your progress
By the pleasure your dumb mind associates with
Finality. When it feels like death you may be
Sure it's not you but what you're well rid of.

That alone is worth ten minutes of drudgery
While sitting still. I think of someone now
Who sees no reason to keep going and no tool
Has he in his bag for fabricating one.

Such a one is surely to be pitied. If I could
Explain to him (or to her) about the background,
The secret wisdom nesting between the rafters
Of the wood shed! – It returns every spring.

If I could point to enhancement due to faith;
Indeed to a liveliness that cannot commence
Except it grates first on the nerves and
Perchance spills a little blood on the tiles.

*

She said I'd be amazed if I knew what all she
Regrets and repeatedly sweeps under the carpet.
She said happiness had nothing to do with it but
The wrong information at each and every turn.

I could not have helped her because I myself
Was swimming against the stream and night had
Set in unfortunately before the other river bank
Came into view, which left me treading water.

It was more or less a case of untimely abstraction
That meant the broken wing had to be seen to first
Prior to love being allowed to make sense,
Plus the shabby attitude – and she was moody.

So we stared into the fire and we recollected
Past investments, when first we bought the chickens
And she helped me build a little wooden house
And a wire mesh run for them to peck under.

We made the quarry safe for the children.
Unexploded shells, gunpowder sticks,
Also mantraps lay concealed in the bracken.
Oh, we laughed a great deal in those days.

Now we have it easy and some bad habits
Have crept in, some addictions to brutishness,
Unwillingness to apologize for cutting new teeth,
The reluctance to cope with unusual flesh.

One does feel cornered as soon as one does not
Take care of one's soul, that subtle indicator of
Which way the wind blows and should we hoist sail
Or would we be smart to start the motor.

This may be the time for going over the top.
What I am doing now lends focus to nearly
Any damned thing that arrives by air or
Springs ready-armed from the blood stream.

Yes Ma'm, I have it now, sorry for making you
Wait. Not that I could have satisfied you
Earlier, it's not entirely in my hands, this
Creativity, especially when love is involved.

Now I rise to my feet, stretch arms to the
Heavens, I'm glad to be alive. Not much more
Is required, really, I shall continue like this,
Leisurely advancing good spirit again.

Possibly a lot needs to be seen to now and
What between sprigs of asparagus and fine dining
I let the legislation fall into place. Perhaps
One should always deal with regret most speedily.

*

42

Unless, of course, one slides along,
Can't think of anything being wrong.
The belly is full, the bed is soft,
The sun is drawing us aloft,
The skin is safe, the belly is full,
What is this indeterminate pull?
I wish I knew but I can't think,
Except my usual meat and drink.

A mild dissatisfaction perhaps with one's
State of being, if one can point to that without
Losing track of the thing that counts:

That feeling of lethargy which cries to be
Objectified perhaps, however all the while
Felt and felt still and again because
It has to occur to us that we can make something
Out of it. Our Growth demands it.
Again, do we have the choice to grow or to stagnate?
Not sure? Stagnate for a while. Does it suit you?
Any more questions?

You encircle it, you curse it, push I away,
Drink coffee, seek excitement, sensation but
Good heavens! Too much sensation causes this.
It's time to get down to business.

Whatever you do, do it as if it were the only thing
You could do just then. And keep at it.
Don't look back. Don't depend on visible output.
During the evident pauses there's most progress.
This is shocking! Suddenly an outpouring –
Followed by – once again – stagnation.
However consider you've moved a thing;
And not just up the hill to roll down again.
Tackle indifference too, if it arises.
These are all treasure troves, negatively advertised.
Regret, resentment, apathy – study these in detail;
Not at the moment because you are busy.
You are on the scent of spiritual augmentation.
You may be composing, so you place your entire trust
In that next phrase, that next harmony or melodic line.
Never ask: do I like this. That leads nowhere.
Afterwards you will get your chance.

Is growth inseparable from work?
Let's put it this way: they imply each other.

You want an increasingly dependable
Foundation for you existence.
You want to create a work for the benefit of others.
You want more power, always more power
Both for being able to do more good
And for being strong enough to withstand
Shocks to your system, setbacks;
Shorter reaction time to the elemental undertow.

Important to keep in mind that our human nature
Is organic, is a power-block, is live energy that
Needs to pour itself into ever greater, ever more
Sophisticated, ever more communally beneficial
Ends. If we do not supply our human nature with
Opportunities for disporting itself, above all
Exemplifying itself, it ails. It sickens.
I have mentioned that recently.

*

43

Find your own individual way of accommodating
Your human nature. That is your business, not anyone else's.
Take time to do that. Often. Perhaps think of your human
Nature as something that needs to be fed, to be facilitated –
In short, it needs something to do or it
Reminds you that it has nothing to do.
That does not feel good. Not nice. Over time it can
Feel like the bottom has dropped out of you existence.

Your human nature needs limits.
It resents being left in chaos.
It regrets being ignored
Never forget about your human nature
Because that is where your god is at home.

And choose your god carefully.
Go right to the top, if you can.
There are gods, and there is god.
Choose god.
Then the gods will eat out of our hand.

The home god makes for himself in your human
Nature is your soul, you may as well know that.
The modern gods want you to sacrifice your soul to them.
Avoid them. Wish them well but avoid them.
Don't fuss. Even the fact that you exist –
This before you do any work –
Makes a good difference to your environment.
However it must be existence
Based on your human nature.

* * *

44

Now that we have some notion of growth as I imagine it here,
We should be able to illustrate the role that is played by us
As creative facilitators and as cheerfully suffering functionaries.

So for example the poet must always tread a fine line between
The spirit that operates in darkness and what he himself knows,
Otherwise the manner of expression is bound to explode in his face.

Nature, then, is birth and we have to make up our mind
Are we glad to be born or can we never quite make our peace with it
And so we espouse abstraction to the point of self-annihilation.

Against that, is birth arbitrary and are we the accidental outcome,
The inappropriate fact and the accumulation of problems
That define us, before we begin, as organically inconsequential?

Why are you here? I ask so that you may consider asking.
Are the woods so dark, is the fog so thick that you cannot make out
The slender shoot that springs from the warm soil in May?

If something stirs within you and if you now call it emotion
Or desire, that's even better, then let the following question be:
What is the purpose of it? Why me rather than someone else?

The reason for that is that most initial stirrings are raw,
Not intended for immediate consumption, hence that short pause
To let your god know you're available and ready for business.

This is another way of saying: Remain aware that the elements
Show their face within you but concealed behind a mask
For which you are responsible, so accept the responsibility.

So practice pause and reflection when first you begin to grow.
Look how the babe's members long for loving containment.
Of course I mean the time now of your adult growth in spirit.

Wrongly we think of spirit as enhancement and stimulation.
That is the ancient persuasion. History has moved on.
Today we do well to account for spirit as physical being.

Any and all spirit? Oh no, not by a long shot.
If you want to survive as a human being, you'd better be selective.
The popular world is a mass of disembodied spirits.

Discernment is of the essence. Only ask quickly
Where a given spirit leads. Does it merely wish
To make of your human body its permanent habitation?

If so, be advised to deny it its wish by kindly explaining
How you are otherwise committed. However make no effort
To persuade a lame mule to behave like a fiery stallion.

Know that your god exists in the flesh; that's the end of your worries.
Try to understand that good spirit clothes itself with your body.
Thereafter it will not allow disembodied spirits to annoy you.

However it will let you know when the time arrives for growth.
Now you may well experience the anguish of the favourite child;
The loneliness of the orphan, the rootlessness of the waif.

Now it shall become evident whether you have what it takes
To see through these masks which, due to your primal inertia,
Have superimposed themselves upon the urges of good spirit.

"You shall exist," says your god, "in spite of your vile inclinations.
Come out of ourself and embrace the reality I have planned for you.
Do it in your own way – but do it, or suffer the consequences."

Oh, that sounds ever so heartless! And this is the god of love
Who imposes his will on his creature as though it had no will?
Something is blatantly wrong here with how we view the truth.

One thing we have forgotten: We are free to deny this god.
Or call it rather a liberty, since freedom without good spirit
Is merely a bald invention and never worthy of the name.

We remain at liberty to say no. I will not believe this spirit.
I reject all interference with me as the god of my self
And I shall remain unmolested by anguish, loneliness and grief.

Free will, plainly stated, this child of modern inventiveness,
Bleats, not quite inaudibly, like a goat snagged in a fence.
Certainly we may take pity, but we cannot turn a goat into a sheep.

*

45

"Even to the ends of the earth" – the wise man knows –
Good spirit blesses our being and doing – relentlessly.
By this I mean that if we believe good spirit
We will not be allowed to fall away from this blessing
No matter how stupidly or ignorantly we behave.
We may take it that even our accidents then have meaning
And if we stubbornly go wrong, we will be corrected.
Now here's the thing that people will find impossible
To countenance, because it goes against their myths:
Anguish, loneliness, grief are all blessings
Inasmuch they draw our attention to merciful good spirit.
In the present work we show how this is so.

Also we make no attempt to convert non-believers,
However we show by personal example what we mean.
This is the best we, in our position, can do –
This present work too counts as such an example.
So really our very first action, as we grow, must be
Repentance, as should be obvious now by all.
The nobility of genuine human being is at stake.
If we wait, before we repent, until our conscious
Acts convict us, we will never cease from being modern.
We repent for what we have done unknowingly
Because we are aware of the nature of our goal.
Also we understand what it is that gets in our way
Right from the start when we make our decision to exist –

Or let us say: – each time we make that decision.
Non-existence now and again confronts us –
This is not something we readily like to admit.
However as an exemplary act, this very repentance
May be precisely what is required in our community.
We should not suppose that existence initiates a standard
Uphill climb from the time we first come to realize
That humanity, as the essence of being, frequently returns
to pay a creative visit to its place of birth.
Each time, however, we will surely comply more capably
And more in tune with what, at the time, is required.

We need to imagine ourselves, in our adult maturity
And in our community, as ethically procreative.
On one hand, as time passes, we become more competent
And on the other we are entrusted with greater tasks.
Gladly we choose to shoulder each other's burdens.
Certainly one of the heaviest burdens we encounter
Is existence itself blocked by elemental reaction
In a member of our community. We ourselves react
And reject that person as too dangerous. Then we realize

What we have done and shame brings us around.
It would have been so much easier to cajole him
With kind words, helping him to ignore his problem,
Then walking away. I think we would be amazed,
If someone now were to bring to our attention
What a life-giving opportunity we just then forfeited.
So once the ability to repent is in our tool-kit
We do well to use it also on behalf of our friends.
Of course where someone is committed to non-existence
We will find ourselves casting the dust from our feet.

*

46

Universal order, the logos, the kingdom of heaven,
Or instead the popular conceits, public and private,
Vain insistence on deserved advantage of self –
The unending, bitter argument for self-justification,
Only barely concealed by the social niceties –
We need to make our decision, the die is cast,
The times are over when we may linger on the sidelines
Weighing the pros and cons, enjoying the cheap
pleasure of dithering, entertaining our complaints
to make ourselves seem so much more deserving.

I advertise the beauty of god's grace.
If that were all, who cures me of my arrogance?
The hunger of the heart is justification.
What does that mean, exactly, to crave justification?
Did we not at the start identify
That element against which we reacted
As justice? So is justice not universal?
Are we to think of god's hand as a myth?
Or are we to distrust the truth revealed to us
At such times as when we know ourselves in god?

Our reaction to god's justice is indifference;
This I have learned, and I recall it now
To teach that truth to my indifferent mind,
Namely that if I intend to overcome
My arrogance, my insistence that I'm right,
I'd best learn quickly how to be meek and mild.
Humility must seem shameful to the devil,
Not to the one who seeks positive alteration
Of his condition: cursed self-righteousness.
Oh for the wisdom now of a little child!

*

47

The logos – are we clear about what that means?
A teaching needs a teacher and by some accounts
Logos refers to both. That may well be
More than we can account for with our senses.
However some can see only what appears
While others see the root of their sensation
And certain secrets are then revealed to them
Which justify investment of the heart
(I mean the heart as organ of affection)
In human being. Now there's a novel thought!

Knowledge of human natural affection
Has been for years mistaken for romance
And Amor, that untrustworthy trickster
Delivered up his sexual fantasies
To ridicule when the logos came along.
Also he took barbaric liberties
And these the saintly angels held against him.
They charged the little blighter with cupidity
And censored poetry written in his name.
That put the kibosh on all sexual fondness.

Time and again I'm fired up inside,
The poet must confess that sort of thing,
I speak to my beloved not at all
As if I wished her well but more as if
I wanted her to mother or admire me;
It's most peculiar. As you would expect
I get a look that speaks a thousand words,
None of which mean that she is pleased with me.
I put it down to the silly male in me
And make adjustments. Every day a lesson.

Then too I have in mind that not that long ago
Our love was youthful still, often we hugged and kissed
As if we were in love; affection knew no person.
One spirit moved us both in ways that gave us joy.
I think at those times then we little cared for others.
We seemed absorbed in how the pleasure of this love
Took thought of self away, but also thought of the other.
Thought then asserted itself – and so did pain divide us.
It took a while for us to learn this painful lesson:
Thou shalt not fall in love once thou hast learnt to love.

It might be right to say: The logos questions
Our readiness for every stage of growth
And dictates change where change is of the essence.
It urges us to make some preparation
At times, for what – we have no way of knowing
Until we are committed to the move;
Often then we are filled with gratitude.
The logos is the master of our growth,
We turn to it when some uncertainty
Enters our soul, some pain without its cause.

The logos, when that entity exists –
(it does not always, being oft in abeyance,
Perhaps to teach us freedom of our ways
If we begin to cling to it for advice) –
When it exists we may perceive it stands
For universal order – but in progress.
These two then would inform of their affinity:
The universal order and the logos;
And we may learn to view the two as one.

*

48

Kingdom of heaven – rather than kingdom of earth:
The emphasis is on the change of venue.
Heaven is where good spirit has its home
Within our soul – we do well to remember it.
No change so great as that to another kingdom.
Not that the two could ever be at war,
For when our thought and sense is heaven-centred
No kingdom of the world finds fault with us,
For we behave most orderly and logical.
Our trouble starts when we let the two overlap.

The king who rules this kingdom is known to us,
Especially if we grew up in a Christian country
And made some effort to inform ourselves
Of what his rule and what his law amount to.
There's nothing quite so exciting as this knowledge
And soon we learn to cope with this excitement.
We have the Gospels and the Acts to inform us
And many letters by some early believers
In god and Christ, especially Paul of Tarsus,
A man of noble heart and magnanimous mind.

For centuries have we heard of the kingdom of heaven
And wondered, this way and that, what does it amount to.
Of course there are those whose doubts have been erased
By sufficient dogma and sufficient justification thereof.
Also it helps, if we are not sure of something,
To preach it loudly to a public, as if we were sound.
Thereby we may gradually convince our selves.
The problems is, that our selves have a way of reneging
When the chips are down. Then, when we're tired out
By all that preaching, our kingdom just falls apart.

It seems to this present writer it no longer matters
Where we go for our knowledge, as long as we find it.
Myself I always return to the European tradition,
To this melting-pot, namely Jerusalem, Rome and Athens.
The study of civilizations is not my strong point –
I cannot quite take to progress by way of civilization.
However the author's ideas have to be filtered
Through the writer's present opinions, convictions and beliefs.
Those are the two essential poles of genius;
The electric charge flickers from the one to the other.

Kingdom of heaven, logos, universal order –
Each of these complexes is backed by a mighty tradition
And a diverse array of scholars feeds on the fallout.
Scholarship – well, I confess I cannot quite take to it.
I cannot begin to admire that killer instinct
That needs to eradicate whatever adheres to the truth.
On the other hand, I ask myself, what does he mean by beauty?
It's a sobering thought. I have half a mind to pursue it.
In order to come up with a fair representation of what I mean
By beauty and truth in comparison, I have to settle down
To some self-examination. Here I come up against genius
As the principal, productive motor, powered by the elements
As available in terms of what I mean by world environment.

(It appears that the spiral has performed yet another revolution.)
Genius dreams its way through the maze of what is given.
The visions of genius allocate areas of significance,
Of relevance to contemporary humanity here and now.
But genius itself is not something we can take for granted.
In fact, there is no such thing as genius in itself.
This is an insight for which I congratulate myself –

For having the perspicacity to be able to sustain it.
As insights go, this one rumbles in my stomach.
I wonder, have I swallowed rocks and not little goats?
Or perhaps the rumbling, like coals delivered into the cellar,
Is nourishment from headquarters, ready now for consumption.
(I'm afraid these lines are getting longer and longer.)
Perhaps I am trying to turn the spiral into a circle
Or into a straight line, both of which would defeat my purpose,
Which is ever to offer new life to those who desire it.
So is beauty truth and truth beauty, period?

> This 'memento mori' cribbed from a Grecian urn –
> Itself the maggot of a morbid poetic mind,
> Preoccupied with the fading of its after-life,
> Instead of sponsoring real life here and now,
> Spotting the little deaths along the way –
> Lovely good spirit's merciful corrections –
> Should but remind us that our victory is won.
> All this from my unclouded contemplation
> Of "beauty is truth, truth beauty", which shall now
> Be shredded – to make room for what I mean.

I view the world from where good spirit moves
In human being. World, from here, is beautiful.
That we are able to perceive the world
As beautiful, is god's move on earth as truth.

Hence 'truth and beauty' is simultaneous being.
The one without the other is unthinkable.
Yet beauty is not truth, nor truth beauty.
It makes no sense to say that world is true,
Nor is a human being always beautiful.
Yet there is falsehood's mask and tempting beauty.

'Man' is the Christian type, the modern maker
Of his own fortune. He bestrides the globe
Like one who has the intention to be God
And at the same time what he knows and does
Good spirit cannot recognize as love –
And therefore man must fail in his ambitions.
The fact that man is modern is his downfall.
Himself he must experience as divided,
So what he knows and understands as world
Must bear within its heart that same duality.

The modern beauty cannot be conceived
As human-natural, so we think 'out there'
Something must have attributes of beauty
Which can be counted and accounted for.
Contemporary beauty rests, all one,
In world where we are able to conceive it,
So that we may experience it here within
As beauty without doubt, without temptation.
Not all have what it takes to overcome
Attachment to the thousand threadbare things.

The modern truth is difficult to define
Because it must by sign and witness be
Attested to – even when its shadow
Is cast by pictures and by grand designs
Which last while daylight lasts. Therefore we seek
Contemporary truth, for it outlasts us,
Residing, as it does, in one who shares

His entire being with each one of us,
And so all falsehood quickly is revealed
And quickly neutered by a single word.

I sometimes think the entire world is false
When I hear people talk. And yet they take
Such interest in the outside of the world,
The evanescent skin of this duplicity,
As if by lying something could be gained.
It's true, we lie, when we ignore the truth
And we are ugly when we 'beautify'
The bits and pieces of our interim state
That would respond to spirit-transformation
If we but probed our reason for being around.

*

49

I wonder if this might be the time to continue with
An explanation of how the truth came into the world
And made endless world possible as experience.

This is such an interesting topic that most people
Would probably give their eye-teeth to find out
Exactly what happened and when.

As a child I was always unhappy that I existed
In a world that seemed to me riddled by doubt,
By bad feeling and bad intention.

It might be a good idea for the sake of readers
Who by now are getting tired of strenuous thinking
If I introduced some personal experience.

I was born with my head in the clouds, my feet in
Clay and my hands tied behind my back,
Ready to take on life.

Eagerly I asked all around where I might
Find some life so that I could test myself
But people shook their heads and walked off.

Subsequently I developed some shocking complexes.
On my second birthday I demolished my cradle
And set fire to my parents' house.

Naturally they traded me in for a robot
Who was well behaved, as you can imagine,
The delight of friends and visitors.

I entered school as a robot and won
Numerous prizes for my exemplary behaviour
But also for how I used my brain.

This is where the fun began, because my brain
Operated in reverse, through no fault of mine,
And I managed to keep that well hidden.

For example if someone boxed my ear
I always suspected there must be good reason for it
So I shook his hand and thanked him.

Or if someone called me a fool or an idiot,
I thought right away to myself: True enough,
It has often occurred to me too.

So if truth be told, I made no enemies,
On the other hand I made no friends either.
Maybe you understand that. I can't.

At the ripe age of twelve I began to wonder
why was I always waiting for something?
And what, exactly, was I waiting for?

I eagerly threw myself into what was in those days called
Nature, I mean mountains and meadows and lakes.
I climbed, swam and picked flowers.

In winter I played ice-hockey and a puck knocked out
my two front teeth. This upset me to the point
where I decided to start reading books.

What I found out then shook me to my soul.
I learned that letters, written down on a page,
Could make a person aware of who he was.

So I learned who I was and it pleased me no end.
I expected people would be pleased too
But oh, I was wrong about that.

They said: Nobody cares the least who you are.
They only care about what they can turn you into,
So please, sort out your priorities.

Grief. Nothing but grief. That was me then.
I lowered my head just a little out of the clouds
And this made me feel a little better.

I also sucked my feet out of the clay
And took to riding a pony across the prairie
Of western Canada, where I lived then.

I discovered I could steer that pony with my thinking.
Which was just as well, because my arms were still tied
Behind my back. Hardly anyone ever noticed.

For the next ten years I continued to go to school
While the cords that tied my hands grew moist and pliable
From the sweat. I sweated a lot.

I also frequently wept during those years,
Maybe because there was no one to embrace –
Not that I could have if I'd wanted to.

I went out with girls. It was the thing to do.
They lost interest when they realized I was not into ownership.
I didn't blame them. That was not my way.

Then, one day, I was sitting on a toadstool,
I was crocheting a doily, a birthday present for my mother,
When a man stepped up to me and said:

"That's marvellous how you can crochet behind your back!"
Imagine my astonishment. He had actually noticed.
Then he said something I'll not forget.

He said: "Try to prepare yourself for a great occasion.
Somebody has noticed you and thinks you might be useful
For showing people how to draw breath."

Thank you very much, I said. I'm glad you warned me.
Then he stepped behind me and loosened my fetters.
He more or less untied my hands.

For some time I had no idea what to do with them,
So obviously in front of me, where everybody could see.
It took all of ten minutes for me to learn.

Obviously I looked forward to that great occasion
And by golly when it came I was glad I'd been warned
Because it knocked me for six, I can tell you.

I'll tell you now what happened. A big man with an axe
Brought it down on my head, sharp end first,
So that my brain was exposed to the heavens.

I should really have warned you and not come right out
With something so horrible, but there you have it.
For a week I walked around in a trance.

Then gradually it dawned on me that the living truth
Was no longer a thing of the past, but a quantity
That needed to be taken account of.

This changed my entire point of view about the world.
I no longer saw it as a cesspool, a veil of tears,
Something to which I had accommodated myself –

But as endless experience with not a bad bone in it.
So I'd been right all along, that the badness lay in me –
And now I also knew who had put it there.

Forgive and forget. The best way forward.
Here I am now, with no bone to pick
With the past; all gratitude and appreciation.

*

50

The versification of content is no mean feat.
Making the two one, that is my intention.
That is the essence of the act. As far as I can see
One cannot do better. Of course one can do different.
How one decides, this is one's personal destiny.
We can learn from each other how to be genuinely ourselves.

*

51

Sometimes I like to think while I'm lying down.
At other times standing, or walking, is an advantage.

*

52

Now at one time the truth was not in the world.
This may be understood in a variety of ways
And I do take it that understanding is important,
However it depends on what we stand under.
We cannot understand the root of a problem
Because under the root there is earth en masse
And mass is devoid of rule or key.

So the truth was not in the world, which implies
That the world, to all intents and purposes,
Was not as it is with the truth in it.

58

Sometimes it helps us to understand if we simplify.
At the time when the truth was not in the world,
Where was the truth? Was it not perceived?
This is how the rational mind disports itself.
The thing is, once we begin to think clearly,
We can no longer recall how we were confused,
So it's best to concentrate on what we see clearly,
And this, at the moment, is the world with truth in it.
I can see that clearly and I call it world
To emphasize the physical reality of the world
And its endlessness. World is truly without end.
Once we have begun to worship in reality,
As I do at the moment, we think of 'the' world
As a myth, in other words as of something cast aside
And now no longer worth mentioning.

An equally interesting question, of course, is:
How was the world different when suddenly
There was truth in it, and what were the implications?
Now imagine the difference between a finite mass
Such as a seed-corn before it's sown in the ground
And the sprout that appears above the earth's surface
After the seed has lain in the soil
Under suitable conditions and at the proper season?
The shoot appears and then it divides.
Then it divides again and again
So that every division marks a new step forward.
Some stand by and say: The seed should reproduce itself.
They see that it doesn't, so they walk away.
Others are reminded by the branching plant
That maybe they themselves ought to be branching,
And this annoys them, so they cut the plant down.
Still others take care of the plant and are delighted.

The fact that they begin to branch within themselves
At first disconcerts them but then they realize
That this is the effect of the truth all around
And how silly would it be to reject the truth!
At first they regret, they resent, they're indifferent
But as soon as they notice, they pull themselves up short
And they love instead – and so it goes well with them.

I dare say you noticed just now as we rode
The spiral onward on its determined course
How we passed, once again, curving widely,
far down below us, our point of departure?
This lets us know we are on the right track.

*

53

So how did the truth come into the world
And change into world for those who understand?
So far I have only mentioned how it came
Into *my* world – like a violent storm.

For an answer to this question we must allow history
To speak to us in a voice devoid of scorn,
In a voice pregnant with mystic meaning,
In a voice calculated to transform.

What we hear when we lay our ear to the past
As though an infinite number of centuries
Forced us to believe that time stands still
Except to punish our mockery –

What we hear is a prolonged wail of agony,
As mankind strips its flesh of all covering
To express to whatever gods might have substance
Its own pitiful need of substance.

How can we not feel compassion for mankind
As it lurks in its caves, its pyramids, its tombs,
Searching even among the dead for comfort;
In its art, for believable substance!

Think now, if we ourselves are moved
In our hearts by the way mankind seems tossed
From pity into terror and back into pity,
How much more so the god of all gods?

Here we have merciful good spirit, creative
Of gods and men to the ends of the earth
And as far as man's mortal nature allows,
This time-worn, cracked vessel.

Every culture imaginable has its god
Or its gods, and all reflect popular attributes,
As you would expect, and as a consequence
How can the truth find entrance?

When we say 'the truth', you see, we mean
Something that drains all being of error
And shows one single substance where god
May attach universal affinity.

Merciful good spirit, rarely appreciated
In ancient times, and then as if unapproachable,
At last enters a child of mankind:
Behold, the first true human being!

So this is how it happened, two-thousand years ago.
The first true human being lived
Among people of the earth and suffered the consequences.
The record of that experiment is available to us.

The merciful, creative suffering of those consequences
Is what we mean by that true human being's resurrection;
In other words his development and evolution out from
Among the dead to the truly living.

Hurray, we have him now, here within and among us,
The king in his kingdom, the master in his workshop,
The logos personified, the centre of the universal
Order and our problem is solved!

You say you can't believe this? I can well believe it.
Certainly I myself had the wits to question it
And out of my intensely doubtful integrity
Was born the true insight that I needed.

A young man at the time, eager for the truth,
And vouchsafed an experience of merciful good spirit,
I speedily commenced upon my own resurrection
And I set my example for others.

If someone supposes that by repeating these words
He will make himself secure against death and disease
He will learn that dogma, which is truth as opinion,
Is powerless when death makes a move.

Only the truth that is physically ingested
And imbibed as the personal truth within us,
Which is Jesus of Nazareth, as the Christ, the Messiah,
Builds up our fundamental substance.

Here in a nutshell now we have before us
Elementary resistance, regret and indifference,
All of which amount to that shame we feel,
The offence of being challenged by that person.

Quickly let us love, that we may have the advantage
Over all those spirits that plan our downfall.
Quickly let us act, that we may set the example
Of a true human being at work.

* * *

54

Now I will turn to a subject
That is dear to me because it touches on the work-ethic
Of genius as the true, human-natural principle of creation.

Certainly I have no intention
Of saying the final word about anything here,
Especially since genius, is the epitome of personality.

No one should speak of love
Unless at that very moment he loves.
Otherwise he fishes in a cistern. The same goes for genius.

So we do well if we begin
With an explication of human nature
As fully re-established and outwardly creative and productive.

We grow up in the modern world
Among modern people with modern ideas
And this must eventually cause us to question our being.

No wonder, since humanity refuses
From birth to be strapped into fashionable armour
Of the sort that cannot be depended upon during combat.

So the human being exerts itself
Primarily against that which is less than human;
As a result it learns about death, suffering and life.

It may take quite a while for us to realize
What we're up against on the earth among those who tell us
That they too live, suffer and die like ourselves.

We try our best, of course,
Not to rebel, not to make a fuss,
But eventually the sheer weight of our accusation betrays us.

We have to take a stand, but gradually
It dawns on us that the language presently at our command
Is unsuitable for expressing all that we feel and think.

Those who listen to what we say
Pick up the exact opposite of what we mean
And the crowds of those who agree with each other exclude us.

What counts is that we reflect
On ourselves to decide, do we have what it takes
To carve out a world of our own, no matter how small.

If we do, our resurrection can begin.
We learn to interpret the malice, the resentment,
In fact whatever is painful – as useful for our growth.

Let's face it, we want eternal life,
We've had a taste of it, we can get more,
So we have to come out from among those who
                                steadfastly refuse it.

We suspect the truth will see us through
So we have to learn how to cloak the truth
So that it will stand on its own two feet of concrete.

For ourselves we need to wear a mask,
However among those who surround us there are some
Who do have the will, but lack the courage to come out.

We ask ourselves now, is there something
We can do to encourage the children of good spirit
And teach them the decisions that will help them exist and grow.

Certainly if art is our metier,
We want to know is true art possible or should we
Limit ourselves to comfort, to sympathize and to entertain?

Whatever we do, we will not
Try to excite, to horrify, to sensationalize,
To titillate, to tempt, to appeal to the dead of soul.

Neither will we be critical
Of those who do those things because
It is not up to us to judge the people of the earth.

Human beings value
their soul, while those who prefer to do without,
We call people, which is not the conventional use of that word.

So simply ask yourself now,
Is it your wish to be popular and materialistic
Or do you value nobility, honour, respect.

*

55

Beyond that the quest for 'true art'
Has led us who are modern into diverse straits.
From the time that we first realized that something
Within us was not quite as we would like,
We found ourselves running from one side of the ship
To the other, in the hope of discovering the last
Building block that would allow us to complete the edifice.
When the ship capsized we found it on the sea-bottom.

The definition of human nature
As rational perfection within,
Altered the entire picture for artists and art-workers.
Nature always had to be trimmed,
Squeezed, drawn and quartered, idealized
By talented individuals because nature was not human.
Come to think of it, it had very little to do with birth
And much more with changing shapes and forms.

Then came along the human being
Who decided that he in himself was natural,
Informed by faith; by the dying Christ

Depleted of all death-hunger –
And now genius stretched its wings.

All genius needed was finite limits
In order to escape from his procrustean bed.
We human beings – look how we celebrate
The perfection of our soul, our thirst, our weaknesses!
This we call art now is basic communication
From god to potential gods, from spirit
To spirit, both enveloped in justice.
Please let us have no more magical things.
Those who wish to be moved, to be transported,
Let them take a taxi. Leave our emotions,
Our passions, thoughts and feelings alone.
Never interfere with the grown-up business
Of women and men who look to art
For resurrection-recipes; for evolution-hints,
From art-workers. – Artists, on the other hand,
look into a mirror when they try to
represent the world they might know.

Human nature marries world
And art-works are the happy children.
World experience breeds genius,
Also known as the son of man.
If we cherish human being,
Being greater than ourselves,
And we die to our own weakness
In the Christ we know within,
Then we live the life eternal
Within life-supporting bounds.
Human beings love all beings,
Intellectual as that sounds.

*

56

Would it be right to say that art
Is an extension of human nature?
Would it, in turn, be right to say
That human nature depends on art?

The way we question our environment
Dictates how we end up living in it.
We can move annoyances out of the way
Or we can question why they annoy us.

*

57

It happens that you have a headache,
So you sit down with it and you ask:
"Where do you come from? What do you have for me?"
Patiently you wait for it to respond to your question.
Existence in growth is pain-staking at times.
You do persevere with that pain: "You behave,
As though I were in your way, preventing you from
Delivering a message or performing an operation."
I realize I am frequently slow on the uptake
Or I rush ahead to impose my point of view.
At the same time I know, as do most people,
That misfortune arrives on our doorstep
To draw our attention to something other than itself.
A sore finger suggests I draw out the sliver.
A sore tooth reminds me its time for that filling.
Also we suspect that a pain ignored is a pain doubled.
Also there are so many different kinds of pain
And all of them – let it be said again –
Are growing pains of one sort or another.
 Grief, for example, aggravates the growth of the soul.
(I might have to say that three times to be understood.)

Pain draws our attention to past behaviour.
Intense pain lets us know we'd better hurry
To find out where we've gone wrong in the past.
Well, all this is partially true. One sure-fire response to pain,
Which clears the mind and facilitates the heart,
Is what we have mentioned before, namely repentance.
A new, not a modern, definition of repentance is:
A change of heart in the direction of
Confession, humility and courage.
Let's take a closer look at those.

*

58

Confession: I freely admit, to whoever cares to know,
That in terms of growth I am fallible.
We cannot be prepared for all that might happen to us.
Now and again I will not only get a surprise
But an unpleasant one. Therefore
It makes no sense for me to beat myself up about that.
However there is bound to be that unmistakeable sense of failure.
Only those who have put their foot down and said:
I refuse to grow! will never experience that sense of failure.
Bless them. They have embraced death with a will.

That sense of failure is dealt with in terms of repentance.
When it comes to growth we do well to be perfectly practical.
We will always want to know what works and what doesn't.
Now if we are guilty of having made a mistake
Repentance will work, because it invariably
Includes a secret apology to god.
Since we know our god as merciful good spirit
That secret apology suffices,
And since we're honourable at heart,
Our apology includes: I will try to do better next time.
So goodness me, repentance even includes

That willingness to learn new tricks!
It seems we're on to a good thing here.
Most of the time, however, there's no need at all
To try to work out where we've gone wrong.

But surely you are bound to repeat the same mistake?
Well, let's just review our overall mindset here.
We embrace the sort of human progress we call growth.
In the absence of good spirit the growth we mean is
meaningless.
To be and work in the presence of good spirit is our goal.
We are committed to this for life, not only on Sundays,
So is it likely we'll be dishonest in our intention to improve?
I'd say that nowadays we cannot even repent properly
Unless at the same time we 'seek the kingdom of heaven'.
We apply to the logos for our next move.
We appreciate our presence in the universal order.
(I do my best to stay clear of dogma.)

As for humility, I dare say at least a degree of it
Is required before we can confess or repent.
Are we not bound to see ourselves in a true light
As soon as we step into that little space
That is reserved for us and only us
In case we should ever wish to question
Our reason for existing on this earth?

It takes courage to be humble and equally
Courage that is real and true requires humility.
Both of them depend on confession.
Whether we suddenly find ourselves at our wits' end
Or exposed on a peak of arrogant self-righteousness,
This triad of confession, courage and humility
Is liable to work wonders for us – if we prefer.

*

If we define genius as human nature
Directly in line with elemental nature,
We can see why there is no such thing as 'a genius'.
Or rather, let us say that 'a genius' would be a thing
And not a being. I mean: Not a human being.
We have to come to terms here with what would
Impede our growth. So why not
Have a go at distinguishing the being
From the thing. That is always useful.
A genius would be someone who has cosseted
His nature separate from other natures
And he arrives at an image of himself
As select, and elect – while being derelict!

I agree, it does sound monstrous.
We might as well be aware of what's involved here.
If there were such a thing as a genius –
And perhaps there is, I'm no judge –
Then we might do well to stay clear of it,
Unless, of course, we're on a mission
And have what it takes to revive things.

Perhaps I should repeat here what I've said
Elsewhere about beings and things.
It's a modern ambition, you see,
To turn all beings into things.
The explanation for that is
That beings attract our attention
For the purpose of highlighting our own being,
Which is to say as human beings,
And this is because we, by definition,
Have what it takes to complete
All beings, not only ourselves.

The universe of beings, you might say,
Waits with bated breath
For human beings to clean up their act
So that they can do what they're meant to do,
Which is render all creation whole.
So if you are addressed by some being
Which is bound to remind you of your responsibility,
But you say no, then that being
Is bound to appear to you as a thing.
So there you have your definition of things.
They are products of modern misbehaviour.
It's been going on for two-thousand years.
('Good things' have been going on too, of course.)

Those of us who have what it takes
To revive things, merely create a context
For the being that sleeps within them.
Sounds easy, doesn't it. It's not.
It goes against the grain of modernity.
One is liable to get a lot of criticism
Because, after all, one is challenging
The integrity of the modern way.
Mind you, how else can we achieve
The contemporary resolution that is required
For re-establishing beings in their own right
Except by challenging modernity?

*

60

This takes us right back to the beginning
When the truth first stepped onto the stage
In person; when it brought that sword
Which ever since then has divided
The massive pseudo-reality in two,
So that we identify those two and make them
One, through messianic awareness.

71

The ancient pseudo-reality
Could no longer be sustained.
Right away arose all those
Who took it upon themselves to recreate it
And to demonstrate, by their failure,
That the being they shunned must be allowed.
The initial shunning seems unavoidable.

There now we have quite a lot to take on board.
I never suggested it would be easy.
We can follow this up in the New Testament,
How those who eventually made the greatest
Contribution to the contemporary understanding
Began by denying the truth of it. Those who
Eventually followed, first had to resist.

    Even nowadays there is still
    A huge effort do join
    The two apparent entities
    That do not exist in their own right
    In terms of critical thinking.
    This critical thinking, however,
    Is energized by rejection of truth.

    Clear thinking is not critical.
    It merely replaces confusion.
    We should not suppose that we need to
    Confront whatever gets in the way
    Of our true, personal contributions.
    Criticism merely stirs up
    The modern mind and ill feeling.

So criticism is the understandable reaction,
However much cloaked in bonhomie,
To the unavoidable failure
When we try to explain five
By adding two and two.

Criticism tires us out
And burns us up – selah.

* * *

61

When I think of how I have grown
Over the past sixty years,
What comes to mind to begin with
Is stature, personality and character.
In my youth, if I look closely,
None of these really existed.
As a child I lived in a dream,
As a matter of fact I lived a dream
And dream was stability and comfort.
Mood, too, supported me.
I was neither dreamy nor moody,
But mood and dream sustained me
Through thick and thin during childhood.

The teenage years were problematic.
A new language had to be learned.
A different attitude to existence
Needed to be gradually absorbed
And none of these adjustments were pain-free.
Of course I developed my own
Attitude to the world and this proved
Quite different from the attitude of those
Around me. My parents drew me
In one direction; at school
The emphasis was placed on adaptation
To a system that was barely understood.
I learned to appreciate education
As an eager accumulation of facts.

I 'grew' in the direction of self-esteem
Because I was 'good at facts'.
All in all, as I recall,
As a teenager I did not grow
But I shrank, decreased and diminished.
If I ask myself, did I exist?
I have to say: No, not really.
The dream and mood of childhood
Was turned, by force of the prevailing
Social customs and mores
Into questionable dreams and moods
Which pained and thoroughly confused me.
Swayed between depression and elation,
Badgered by symbols and images
Represented by well-meaning adults,
I skirted the realm of self-hatred.
Music, in the end, saved me.
Also my piano teacher introduced me
To the Rocky Mountains of Canada,
Where we hiked and scrambled and climbed.
I looked down from the top of Mount Temple
And decided that life might be worth it.
I conquered a Beethoven Sonata
And although I never gained much
Satisfaction from performing in public,
I became acquainted with my inward being.
Then I discovered poetry
And realized that we, as human beings,
Can make a contribution to our welfare.
The beauty of the English language
Taught me that human emotion
Could also be divine, if persuaded
To conjoin with inward truth.

In this way I am able to recall
The beginnings of my existence in growth.
In many directions circumstances
Colluded with the needs of the teenager.
Properly mature adults
There were none in my immediate environment,
However from my parents I learned
To respect, to appreciate and to forgive;
No small thing, in a world
That dotes on the survival of the fittest.

That growth commences from within,
This was a tortuous wake-up-call
For the young man who had been schooled
In the various modern disciplines,
None of which presupposed a soul,
Merely a problematic psyche.

What then happens when that psyche
Is suddenly removed and replaced
By infusion of merciful good spirit
Is enough to terrify the timid
And to bring the arrogant to their knees.
This I experienced in person.

So my earliest beginnings of existence
In growth I think of as development.
What commenced then, both
With a bang and whimper, I refer to
As evolution, because this was the time
Of three particular progressions.

These I will name now and specify.
First: production. I discovered
That if I disciplined my mind and my heart
I could create serious works of art,

Albeit on a very small scale at first,
But relevant to my stature as a young man.

By stature I mean how I measured up
To my own expectations of myself
In those particular surroundings at the time.
It's no use pretending that we exist
Anywhere except where we do,
Because that is where the truth begins to matter.

However the capacity for real work
And the stature conferred upon the individual
Distinguishes him in his surroundings
So that he becomes conscious of himself
As radically different from those
Who insist on inertia and decay.

What comes into being for him now
Are the rudiments of his personality,
For he needs to assert himself powerfully
On the side of the living, while the dead
Do not at first take kindly
To the fact that he leaves them behind.

Oh, such a struggle may commence now,
For conscience, humility and pride,
So that kindness shall replace ruthlessness,
That production shall proceed nevertheless
Whatever obstructions it meets with,
So that truth may see the light of day.

Endurance in the face of discouragement,
Insistence on genuine human nature
In confrontation with the established norms,
The rejection of moods and dreams
As ideal building-blocks of a world
That would sacrifice the soul to materialism –

This is what builds early character:
A capacity for holding out
Under diverse strains and distractions,
An unwillingness to give up the ghost
When shame and guilt rear up –
And a readiness for joy nevertheless.

*

62

Production is a great beginning
Because we can get things off our chest.
We learn how to handle our medium
In the way that suits us, without breaking
Too many of the conventional rules
And then we experiment, to discover
The limits of our individuality.

Then, when we encounter hindrances,
Especially within our self,
We acquire the great skill of creativity,
Which implies the ability to overcome
Every sort of ingratitude and grief
That would draw our attention to itself
And away from the creative process.

Creativity therefore implies
Patient cooperation with our soul.
Since our soul is an ongoing infusion
Of ourselves by merciful good spirit,
We can see how every creation
Is bound to comfort and to enlighten,
Whatever else is meanwhile achieved.

Creation in every walk of life
is of the essence, because always, inside,
where our self is ready to assert itself,
we realize, never too soon,

that our redeemed human nature
would persuade us to behave honourably,
while the world is addicted to falsehood.

Also that nature would show us
that we were born with faith,
and that therefore no artificial faith
is needed, it only overlays
true faith with multiple layers
of opinions by interest groups
who need to bolster their fan base.

Imagine now, that instead of a soul,
A psyche is all that is available.
Every outpouring of a psyche
Is but a testimony to our unwillingness
To lay aside our modern prejudices,
To forego our rejection of good spirit,
Of which psyche itself is a sign.

*

63

So just as production will lead
to creation, once we have proven
ourselves competent in that sphere,
so will creation bear fruit
in what I feel persuaded to identify
as the construction of beautiful world.
How this comes about is a mystery.

All we can say at this point
Is that construction of world necessarily
Involves creation and production.
Surely no one expects otherwise.
We find ourselves here at the epitome

Of what human beings need to achieve,
Which is why we call this their resurrection.

Certainly in order to construct world
We must leave the world behind,
So that we may eventually exist
In world without end, in which life
As we know it then, is eternal.
What we build then makes world more accessible
For those who are fed up with the world.

This, now, is our own resurrection.
It is not a resurrection *of* the dead,
But *from* the dead, and this
Is crucial if we hope to understand
Existence in growth, in its entirety
And not only to the point where we die
In expectation of some 'supernatural glory'.

Indeed the entire question
Of what is meant by 'the supernatural'
Is bathed in myths and superstitions,
So that wonder upon wonder, we behold
The fruits of our redeemed human nature
Here and now in the community
Of those with the courage to avail themselves.

*

64

The one who made it possible for us
To venture out from where we might conceal
Our heritage for fear of being punished,
Did himself set the imitable example
Of how, instead of hiding, we might prosper
By shaping the uniqueness of ourselves.
The old adage: 'he died that we might live'

Encourages a sacrificial attitude
That has betrayed the spirit of the time
For centuries and fostered acts of violence
Completely out of character for that man,
Who showed that by not resisting evil
We manage to divert that death-anxiety.
So how we define death is rather crucial.

If he had died, could he be with us now?
No, he lived and he lives
Precisely so that we may live.
Shall we depend, for our definitions,
On the dead? What would be the outcome?
No, by the very way he lived
He overcame death, which is why we say:
He lived and lives so that we may live.

*

65

Once again the spiral has accomplished
A full circle and hovers above its starting point.
We are to exist as carnal creatures
So let us lay aside two things that are
Ingrained in our modern constitution, ibid:
The moralist downgrading of the flesh
(albeit for understandable reasons)
And the hunger, the cravings, of the flesh
(when we cast reasons to the side).

There, that's them gone for the moment.
It's as easy as that, isn't it.
Except, I'm afraid, that it isn't.
Something is involved here that has never,
In my opinion, been thoroughly investigated.
Mind you that's only my opinion.

I intend to look into something here
And little do I care who else has done it.

Behold, I commence from the supposition
That my flesh, by definition, is blessed.
I wonder how that happened. Oh, I know,
It has to do with the achievement
Of the one I mentioned just recently
and may praise accumulate on his head.
Due to his timely interference
In the way humanity was regressing,
We have, within us, what we need
If we wish to celebrate our carnality
As released from demonic bondage.

Well! I say! Is that a fact now?
My friend, you may take it for granted,
All personal evidence to the contrary.
Our flesh, you see, draws attention
To itself for a perfectly good reason.
Our problem is, we fail to understand it.
Our flesh says: Look here, you may take me
As I am, unsoiled, unspoiled.
Get off it, we say, the very fact
That you draw attention to yourself
Is sufficient evidence of your immodesty.

As I mentioned, our prejudice is ingrained.
We know full well that at one time
We insulted the landlord, at another time
We cosied up to his daughter
When she caught us stealing those apples;
She didn't exactly seem unwilling.
Another time we pretended we had fully
Paid up our taxes, which was a lie.
We continue to live under that shadow.

81

'The Church' tells us not to worry,
The debt has been paid, but look,
Those are words, I know what's behind them.
Equally what isn't behind them
Is the personal example I would need,
And not this pretence of a vocation
That separates the man from humanity,
So that he feels free to abuse children
(and that's just one example!)
Because his position places him above them.

There you have one way of looking at it.
What are the temptations of the flesh?
What exactly is being tempted?
And why? To strengthen our morality?
Is goodness, by any stretch of the imagination
A virtue that constructs human beings?
Not on your Nelly, it turns them into
Nonentities with a high opinion of themselves.
We cannot be good. God is good.
We're not meant to be good, but rather
Fully fledged human beings who have no need
To compare themselves to saints and sinners.

*

66

We cannot exist in reality
Unless we have learned the difference
Between our body and our flesh.
We speak of the temptations of the flesh,
Of its urges, longings, cravings,
And its good that we manage to identify these,
But it's ever so wrong to resist them.
Our flesh lets us know in that way
Not that we should indulge in pleasures
But that we are ready for completion.

So what is the way for us to behave
When once again a craving is upon us?
We say to it: Here you are,
Here is your satisfaction.
We say to it inwardly, cheerfully:
How fortunate that you are blessed!
Then we experience the completion,
And that is our body saying to us:
How glad I am to have been recognized.
How fortunate for you that you acknowledge
That your body is an entity in itself
And not at all mixed up with the flesh.
Now your flesh is finally yours
And good for you if you understand that,
Because now you can rise to the occasion
Of life as it floods into you,
Perhaps for the very first time.
And how do you respond to your body
When you notice that it knows what it knows?
You celebrate – it's as simple as that,
And if you don't there are those who will.

By this I mean to explain
How the joy that arrives on our doorstep –
Once we *own* our flesh and our body
As distinct entities rather than
Tinkering with half-baked sensations
And forever regretting our mortality –
How this joy cannot but blossom
And bear fruit of one sort or another;
Perhaps in works you create
Or in the works of someone you love.

*

67

Never forget that you live in community.
When you do live, rather than merely existing,
Your very presence is a blessing for your friends
And a mild sensation for your enemies. Life
Comes to those who are ready
                        as the crown of their existence.
We call it eternal life because
It does not pass. It remains forever
And those who wear this crown of life
Are known as gods, and as sons of god.
Even if you never know such a one,
Never forget what you have learned here.
It will bear you safely through your worst afflictions
And make of your trials things of the past.

* * * * *

The Crown of Eternal Life

What comes to mind first is compassion.
You cannot possibly love one another
Unless you first regulate your existence
And then you have the choice to speak freely
Of how you like to act and behave.
Certainly you will no longer tell anyone
How to go about their daily business
Or what they should be accomplishing.
This is entirely their own concern.

What counts is that you recognize your capacity
For setting an example of life.
Those around you will notice
That this and that works smoothly
When they choose to be in your environment.
And this, after all, is telling,
That your being now is environmental.
You are as you are as you are.
You might like to set that to music.
Or next time you go for a walk
Be aware of how smoothly your steps
Allow you to glide along the tarmac.

You see, there is no need to romanticize.
Even if suddenly hell
Opened up right there in front of you
You may take it for granted you would not
Hesitate but walk right through it
Unscathed by smoke and flame. –
Which is not necessarily an encouragement
To take risks or to court disaster.

*

You have it within you from now on
To uplift others, by your presence,
Out of their immediate doldrums,
Which affords them space to rethink.
Especially those who are in the habit
Of justifying their every move
Will realize there is no longer a need for it.
Of course there was never a need for it,
But now that internal challenge
Brought on by past misdemeanours
Is gradually replaced by compassion.

Such wonderful times you will have now,
Mainly because you are convinced
That everything must go right for you –
And of course you are perfectly right.
Even if you are not particularly
Endowed with intellectual panache,
Never mind, you will get through somehow,
And here's the most surprising thing of all:
No one will envy you your good fortune.
This is because those who know you
Understand very well what makes you tick –
Except that of course they don't.
I have to come back to my description
Of your environmental personality.
As you well remember from your existence,
Which accompanies you along every step,
You have learned how to be a human being
And therefore all beings agree with you.
I refer to an existential concept:
A thing, near *you*, begins to be.

People in general also
Often take a shine to you because
They feel, intimately, that you respect them,
And this, to them is a balm.
Not that people are ever
Disrespected by other than their kind.
Two-thousand years of history
Show this in peculiar fashion,
How groups of people repeatedly
Invent new ways to deplore
And to criticize each other's ways.
Most remarkable, really,
And definitely a great shame,
However there is perfectly good reason for it.
For good spirit to be able to enter
Anywhere and whenever at all,
At least forgiveness must be habitual,
So we must have something to forgive.
This then is cheerfully supplied
By people to one another
Across all the belligerent divides
They create for their static amusement.
I hope there is no need for detail.

All the same, this explains,
Why, for people, genuine respect
Is a balm – and it settles them in themselves,
Which is ever such a bonus, because
Respect is all they ever wanted
And in order to gain it from each other
They undertake such unfortunate schemes
As trying to deserve it, by accomplishments,
By status, gained in ways
With which it is difficult to sympathize.
Again, no need for detail.
What counts is, that you readily supply –

With generosity, impartially and cheerfully,
The balm that must mean so much to them
Because it 'settles them in themselves'.

So there you have one example,
And by no means the least significant,
Of live humanity in action.
Gentle prodding will persuade them
To pass it on to one another:
I mean this genuine respect.
So here you may appreciate again
The effect of environmental personality.
All things will eventually come true
And here you find ourselves in the remarkable
Presence of 'true popularity'.
Who would have thought! Not you.

*

You might say that when you have life,
Compassion is your foremost virtue
And by virtue I simply mean the ability
To do good, in the name of good spirit.

An aspect of compassion I have isolated,
Namely the genuine respect
Paid all beings on earth,
First and foremost people.

What this respect amounts to,
This is an interesting question,
Because, as I mentioned above,
It certainly cannot be deserved.

Therefore you do not ask
Is someone worthy of respect,
But even before you think about it,
You approach that person with interest.

To take an interest in something,
Is a real sign of compassion,
Because right away you need to know
What this being is undergoing.

Certainly you yourself are suffering
As you have learned: when you exist
You come across your elemental rejections
And take care not to reject them again.

You suffer them, as it were, to come unto you,
Since you know they are signs of good world,
Of which you may readily avail yourself,
Because it is your intention to grow.

Your interest then imparts the assumption
That all beings either suffer
Or it would be well for them if they did,
If they are caught up in rejection.

You know that if you yourself
Still linger in unrepentance
Your compassion is only a pretence
And the interest you take is superficial.

Then again how can genuine
Compassion beat critical spirit?
Here, with the best intentions
And interest, we must move aside.

Also, being in pain
Is not suffering and if you insist
That all the world is to blame,
Who will take any interest?

*

Never forget, that now with your life,
In full agreement with your own existence,
Undeniable responsibilities impress themselves upon you.
Believe me, they will take time to reveal themselves to you.

Why not begin by ascertaining a few
Ground-rules according to which
You may sort your experiences while avoiding clinical
Partitioning of intention, of rule and finally of shape.

I am speaking of how you will lay out your program
As you come and go, from within to without,
Returning again to within, each time for the
Final appreciation of your work that relies on communion.

So for example you shall not ignore
What you owe the master and what he wishes
To supply in the interest of his own high connection
Once you have organized what in yourself is appropriate.

* * *

The *seventeen rules of soul devotion*
Clearly apply here and I think we will just
Have a go at delineating a few of them for the love of it
And also because of the life we prize so highly.

*

Number one: The *'construction of world'*, which I mentioned
At the end of the work on existence in growth,
Must surely take precedence, since your overall purpose
Is to let the beauty of eternal life shine forth.

After all, you have endless life to give
And how you give it is entirely up to you,
However it will not be carried into your community
Except with what I will call *'reverence of soul'*.

*

Here, in addition then to construction of world,
You adhere to the second rule, not readily surmised
By those not yet liberated from the modern spirit,
Which likes to produce its own version of a soul.

I suppose we might say, if you hold those two souls
adjacent, the one all anxious to please,
To impress, to insist on itself, to get its own back,
The other most willing to wait for the appropriate moment –

Quickly the life responds to the one
But restrains itself from meeting the other,
Much as you yourself would, if you were approached
By an undisciplined fellow who respected nothing.

*

Now number three: You find yourself urged
Away from the head towards *'carnal awareness'*.
It seems you have spent far too much time
Evolving in terms of united will and intellect.

You know that the modern spirit has misled you
By crowding your carnal consciousness into a corner
And now life reminds you that this must be changed.
You may be astonished by how harsh that reminder can be.

Quickly now practice carnal awareness.
You'd think you were having to lift hundredweights
By the way you sigh and yawn vociferously,
Which shows how reluctant you are to accept life.

I think I might call this a signature experience,
To make it more memorable to the evolving individual.
At first he supposes he is 'under the cosh' –
Like the snooker contestant, exposed to the popular stare.

Again, there's no need to go into detail
As to what exactly is happening, or how.
You feel your habitual attention is rerouted
To what, by comparison, imitates the nether regions.

No wonder, because you've been top-heavy for so long.
Your trunk, your arms, your legs are being addressed.
Muscles, bones, sinews alarm you
And oh the justice of the blood! – and your nerves tingle.

If your head now aches, take it as a sign
That the spirit responsible for all creation
Sees fit to endow you with eternal life
And that this is bound to impair your sense of self.

Poor self hugs itself; what can it lean on?
Is it not even allowed to repair
Its image? No, it's not capable of initiative,
Nor of spontaneity. Self is too busy planning.

*

Which brings us to item the fourth, call it:
'*True spontaneity*' and give it elbow-room.
Here you need to clean your act up post-
haste and then wait. Did I mention that truth is involved?

Aye, but truth has its own axe to grind.
You don't for a moment pretend, with impunity,
That the ball is in your court when all of a sudden now
Teeth gnash, limbs flash, truthfully.

Spontaneous behaviour is true when within
Unimpeachable reason you could not act otherwise.
If you keep that in mind even while you take your bow
In front of an audience, your soul will not get rattled.

Your soul, you recall, is reverential, and this means
The spontaneous truth has quick entry, so
Where otherwise you would have to spring locks and teach
Your mind to attend, you may indulge in the 'dream of Jesus'.

*

This *dream of Jesus* is number five
As I cushion your fall from the modern grace.
Granted, for a time you have existed in growth
But this does not mean that eternal life is a doddle.

What it means is that you are rooted in faith.
Your faith, remember, is human-natural
Not this or that type of intellectual dogma-
drenching that obscures the meek and mild authority.

True spontaneity, as you may master it,
Brings you within range of the dream of Jesus.
Here your organic faculties come to rest
For nourishment, never deserved but freely granted.

How can you tell? Through carnal awareness.
History, now not modern but contemporary,
Confronts you, with the author of love at its centre,
Not entertaining but tender, sweet and affectionate.

Never fear, you will not be captivated.
Your brain, your nerves and senses are all healed.
Keep this recipe handy for a meal
At the time when you fear you may have strained your faculties.

To be more explicit, in this present study,
You may be wise to take on board
That the difference between any dream, while you sleep at night,
And what I here call 'the dream of Jesus' is as follows:

The dream that may vex or enchant you is nothing but a
Reminder to your soul of the nearby psyche,
Which is ready to entertain your sleeping thought
If you should care to substitute deceit for reason.

Now what I mean by the dream of Jesus
Is no such psychic deceptive snare
But even in the light of day it refreshes you
As you call to mind the cause of your good fortune.

And this you do metaphysically now.
Oh what a great mystery is revealed here!
Why, even those who are cursed by their ethnic god,
If they go near the well, they may benefit from this water.

Poetry and music are its twin stream.
The god of wrath perishes on one side,
On the other the god of mercy peacefully thrives
And draws your human love to its own conclusion.

Another aspect of this wonderful mystery
May be revealed to us here at present.
Across the earth, these two millennia now,
All peoples of the earth have dreamt this dream.

Its affinity may be reflected in their religions,
While their wise men, poets and singers, are aware of it.
The great multiplicity do their best to ignore it
While in some it kindles the wrath that curses and destroys.

The few sit on one side of the twin stream –
On the other side the many, who refuse the cup.
And yet, within all, the dreaming is effective,
Is allowed to cause good – or rejects their self-caused evil.

However let us proceed. This dream
Is an aspect of the life available to mankind.
As soon as we use the word 'mankind' we mean
The totality of those who are included in god's plan.

The mighty God who squats upon the nations
Knows nothing of mankind, only of populations
That struggle for sovereignty, for a place in the finite world.
He facilitates those who are willing to sacrifice their souls.

Discussion of this mystery which I have called
'the dream of Jesus' has brought us to where
You may see more clearly now, with eyes that are healed,
All things left in the world to their own devices.

So I come to the sixth item in my list
Which is 'holy sanction', and readily explained.
In all that you do, or prefer to leave undone,
There is life ready to thrive and it seeks your attention.

Whether active or passive, pay attention
To whatever appears unsure of itself.
Things seek the truth, the truth to them is life.
Would you deny them life, for the sake of the truth?

This is a common failure of genius
That life in its nascent form is not recognized.
There is thirst for justice, craving for beauty,
The longing for power to do good – even at a price.

And the price is always some small thing
That has been overlooked, perhaps for an age,
And yet such a small thing was chosen by the power
To complete the worldly order and to make it whole.

To that end then, you who have genius,
And access to the elements of world without end,
What you set your sights on, know it to be worthy
And what you behold, allow it to move you to *compassion*.

*

This will not happen. It must be accomplished.
Only genius can bring it about.
The *holy sanction* of what genius draws forth
From world is the primary task and responsibility of genius.

How would you fancy being 'groomed' by genius?
All that is hidden is being revealed.
We live at a time when this major failing
Of genius is advertised everywhere on the public screens.

The culprit is convinced he did nothing wrong.
Enough said, he did not do the good thing.
He took no responsibility for the attraction of genius
And finds himself pilloried for what he did not actually do.

Similarly a sexually attractive woman,
Unless she accepts responsibility for her effect
On the male gender, she has no right of complaint then,
Except in a court of law, if things go wrong.

We are all of us vulnerable somewhere in our sex.
We are also vulnerable somehow in our nature.
Let him who is gifted with genius, mercifully
Extend this *holy sanction* towards impressionable beings.

Let us assume you are about to meet a stranger.
What is the best way for you to prepare yourself?
Create a space of good will and forgiveness
Within you and become a vehicle of holy sanction.

In that case you welcome life into the equation.
Eternal life operates splendidly.
Are you perhaps not accustomed to think of life
As the quantum-mechanism that drives out what is deadening?

Does it amuse you to think of life
As what you put up with day and night?
Oh aberrancy from one extremity to the other!
Why not just blow out your brains, if that is the case?

Of course it is not. You know that it isn't.
Now how shall you go about keeping in mind
Life's *holy sanction* of what survives on earth
And of all that strives to survive under diverse circumstances?

So much depends on practical application.
However very likely not a day goes past
That does not afford you an opportunity for *holy sanction;*
For the fresh analysis of a need for eternal life.

You may in fact be glad to be reminded
Of that burning need, when least you expect it –
By a hurtful remark, say, from someone you love
Or a stranger's seeming insolence when you asked for a
favour.

Such mishaps testify to a lack of preparation,
And now you know what kind of preparation
Will gain you the sort of response you prefer:
Namely eternal life as *holy sanction.*

There are bound to be those who say: "Why holy?"
For their sake I explain that holiness implies
Not only a lack of precious self-interest
But equally the realization of substantial gain.

Holiness is wholeness as your god sees it
And he gives it his blessing as his first prize
When you have withstood the initial agony
From modern to contemporary; thereafter your human evolution.

The life that you gain, that no one can take from you,
That is what interests you, in comparison to survival.
Gradually it dawns on you that no effort is involved,
Only attentiveness and trust that all will be well.

*

Which brings us to the seventh item on our list,
Which is easy to remember: *'eternal patience'*.
Like all the items that I draw to your attention,
This one too requires solely that you dwell on it.

In other words, once you have housed it in your memory,
When need arises it will suggest itself to you
In one way or another. Your work at the moment
Ensures for your soul magnanimity, for your spirit ease.

Eternal patience eats up the sort of time
That becomes problematic for no apparent reason.
Suddenly you are confronted by an evil force,
But all manner of thing is well because it cannot touch you.

Afterwards you may well wonder what happened
And then your gratitude goes out to him
Who is ever ready to shield you against evil
Even as you allow your being to dwell on his presence.

Due to the popular use of the word
You are bound to wonder what eternity means.
Consider that all things last for a while,
But not forever, so the popular imagination invents –

– what, by comparison, should last forever.
This does violence to the concept of time.
The fact that something lasts implies: for a time.
Whatever is eternal has nothing to do with time.

For example, you compare quality with quantity
And are bound to arrive at a similar insight.
The modern eye sees quantity as separate
From quality, when in truth quantity is perfection of quality.

Similarly you try to compare what is 'good',
And then you speak of what is better and best.
In truth, when it's good, nothing can be better,
Also, when something has quantity, its quality is guaranteed.

The modern mind must help itself out
With likelihood and approximation,
So that it might think of eternal life
As quality of life, when time no longer matters.

The contemporary meaning of eternal life
Implies the quantity of good life,
Bit by bit infused into your modern system
Until the imago emerges freely from the chrysalis.

And so, with eternal patience, the same
Truth holds sway. You shall not think of it
As patience that holds out longer than most,
But patience that implies waiting and praying as one.

Mind you, now, I can just imagine
What my sturdy neighbour will make of this combination
For he waits with one eye on his watch. While he prays,
He will 'say his prayers', perhaps on his knees, at church.

Merciful spirit has not yet touched him,
So how can he possibly know what I mean.
Eternal life is supernatural, he supposes,
For that is what the modern spirit leads him to believe.

He waits for the one who is supposed to come
In the future, perhaps when death has intervened.
The waiting I would teach you here and now
Is the welcoming attitude to the one who is coming now.

Not to forget, one may also follow him.
You may wait for him or you may follow him.
This by itself should help you to ascertain
How he may be reached, depending on who *you* are.

A word about prayer. I will return to it later.
His sword has made the necessary division.
Whatever we do to bring the two together
Is efficient prayer, in the true sense of the word.

*

After 'eternal patience' I would like you to
Consider the meaning of *'human being'*.
An odd request, you will say, because we all know
What it means to be human. Is anything left to learn?

Consider for a moment that there are also
Animal, plant, mineral and elemental beings,
So that clearly we may know five categories of beings,
All of which 'are', and this makes them specific.

Now in order to understand being you need to know
What it means, essentially, to be. In other words,
Since reason allows you to understand beings,
You will conclude that the essence of being is humanity.

Odd as this sounds, it is nonetheless true.
You may have to revise your affinity to that concept.
Humanity takes on animal characteristics in an elephant.
Certainly you may go out of your way to decide what they are.

Humanity takes on human characteristics
In the case of human beings, and this
Should reveal to you an exciting mystery about yourself,
Namely that you are both essentially and existentially human.

This can be true only of *human* beings
And it allows you to compare other beings to yourself.
Your humanity is both essential and existential.
Therefore think of yourself as doubly blessed.

The point is that you are a human being
And that at the same time you also have human being,
Which in turn implies you may lose that human being
Not only some degree but perhaps even entirely.

Thus I must ask you now in sincerity:
How do you identify your human being?
How can you tell you have more or less at a time
Whenever you choose to ask yourself that question?

I believe I will have to help you out here.
Your human being amounts to a capacity
For life – by which I mean eternal life – as a matter of fact
From now on, when I say life, I mean eternal life.

You have more or less capacity for life
Depending on how well you stand with your god.
The spirit which creates and recreates your being
Day in day out, extends to you his own being.

That much agreed upon, what you must ask now is
How can you get better at accepting this offering.
To this we must add that the being of your god
Is love, which is offered to yourself on a daily basis.

You increase you capacity for receiving love
By loving others, both you friends and you enemies.
Merciful good spirit of love and life,
This is how your god allows himself to be described.

*

If now and again I confuse you a little
Don't take it amiss, there's reason for it.
Again I remind of the metamorphosis of the butterfly.
You owe it to yourself to leave your modernity behind –

Or at least to know it as a blatant force
That in all its obvious occurrences challenges
Your conception of yourself as a human being
and always seems more than willing to sacrifice your soul.

Let me put it to you in the following manner:
Life and creativity, as divine infusion,
Stimulate in you a twofold capacity
Called human being – and what, in the end, this amounts to

Is firstly the capacity for living and creating,
Both of crucial importance in your case,
And secondly the capacity for compliance with that infusion,
So that, as you live, your work will become more effective.

You do see, that, when you say *human being* –
You do not yet describe yourself as lifting a finger.
In order to be a human being you must act.
(This, at the moment, is largely a matter of definition.)

If you refrain from loving, god's love
Will occur to you as a burden. If you do not create
God's creativity infused finds you unwell
And upset at having to change our ways and means.

So you do well to take those initial
Creative urges seriously because here
You are being invited to become a human being.
Refusing the invitation is asking for serious trouble.

Alas, like much else, the modern definition
Of creativity and creation needs to be updated.
Genius understands something needs to be overcome.
What good does it do you to love only those you like?

To behave ethically means to do good
Which in turn makes you powerful, more than before,
And in order to do good a creative move is required,
Otherwise the evil reaction will get you down.

Active creation makes room for life,
If you do not shrug off the caring responsibility.
You create with an eye on the truth and beauty –
Meanwhile you are anxious for your fellow human being's welfare.

There is no true creation in the absence of love
And life will not crown the selfish creator.
Would you be a human being, understand what is *human being*:
Mainly the divine/human power to do good.

The path from humanity, the essence of being,
To human being, the power to do good,
Philosophically charted, draws your attention
To life as lived by human beings during their maturity.

When you try to imagine how your humanity
Is the same as that of an animal or a plant,
You can make no progress, until you allow for life
To inform you as only life itself can do.

A king must wear his crown to a purpose.
You live, you human beings, so that life
May be introduced to every being on earth.
It is not in your nature to glory in our existence.

This is probably your greatest challenge,
To live to that particular purpose –
To pass eternal life to all creation,
That every creature may know itself as human.

For this reason alone you have human being,
This genuine power to assist in the completion
Of all that genuinely desires to be,
And therefore also to be aware of its own humanity.

So, for example, when you name something,
A stone, a plant or an insect perhaps,
You are bring it into the realm of human affinity,
Whereupon, from then on, it begins to thrive communally.

If, on the other hand, you label a thing,
Which is how the moderns categorize the world
And they wrongly call it nature – they cause a trend
Of mythification, which fossilizes that thing.

Thereafter that thing is one among ten-thousand
Which have three toes, neither fewer nor more,
Or its sepals are longer than its petals, and its label
Is in Latin – but let's keep in mind: labelling is not naming.

If earth is the breathing organ of the universe –
And this is definitely a useful way to put it
While you decide should you evolve or not –
Then do name beings, rather than labelling things.

You will never get 'nature' under your control,
Nor the earth either, which is fortunate for you.
However you seem to need to tire yourselves,
You chronic assemblers of modern facts and fictions.

*

In relation to what I have told you about humanity,
About human being and a human beings,
The ninth item is *'human nature'*
From the point of view of contemporary philosophy.

You may be aware that contemporary philosophy
Is knowledge derived originally from within
Your organic being, where you follow or tarry
And no one can make you accountable for it.

What a writer of true language presents
Is always acceptable to his own community
However far it reaches – and through it
He extends his community from work to work.

In fact such a writer is always the first
To broker any new truth he discovers
Not to his community but to the world at large,
Whereupon his community extends then.

So human nature is not what you suppose
Happens to you when you look somewhere else
But rather you generally become aware of it
As soon as you look for it in the right place –

– and in the right direction. But this is not easy.
So much depends on how you were brought up
And educated. Was the emphasis mostly on survival
and on how best to leave our mark on the world,

or were you at times persuaded to consider
the welfare of the person standing next to you.
In fact there are those who call human nature
The source of the very truth you were born with.

The modern mind has no intention
To search for the truth, wherever it looks,
Unless by truth you mean subtle distinctions
Made between this appearance and that.

So if your process of evolution has commenced
And you find yourself thrust into a corner of ignorance
As if you had never known a thing,
Why not consider the knowledge within?

Here you will gradually arrive at that certain
'reason of the heart' Descartes discovered.
I don't think he meant romantic love.
He had experienced the boundary of modern intellect.

Now you will probably find yourself asking:
How far do I really want to go in this direction?
How great is my urge to explore my nature?
However here I have to warn you against something.

Either do one or the other, because
If you dabble in the truth and toy with your nature
While clinging at the same time to survival values
You will neither be happy nor will you survive.

So if your redeemed nature interests you
Stick with it, please, through thick and thin.
Personally I believe that soon nothing else
Will hold any water or fill the bill for you.

However, let's face it, you would no be reading this
If your interest were entirely of a critical nature.
The critical nature is not the human nature,
Not to begin with and not in the end.

So take this to heart: The truth will see you through
If you put all your apples into that one basket.
The fact that your nature is not faulty but redeemed
Will dawn on you as soon as you trust it completely.

Your critical nature, when it comes to that,
Is not even human, in the strict sense of the word,
Because 'human', as I pointed out above, implies
Existential growth, and at least development,

While critical spirit is always static,
Frozen, specifically, at the point where otherwise
Evolution would take over. However, evolution
Initially has to pit itself against that restraint.

But do consider now the modern spirit
Which makes a career of arrested development,
So that no one can even contemplate evolution
Without facing that horror, even in himself.

The modern spirit seeks to perpetuate
In those who lend themselves to that energy –
Upon a foundation of massive increase –
Generation upon generation of robots.

Compare it to a horde of frustrated caterpillars
That insist on ignoring and resisting 'the butterfly'
By devouring every morsel of available food
Until the supply runs out and they die.

Of course no such caterpillar exists in reality
Because modernity is strictly a human invention,
And a destruction of humanity based on 'free will'.
However, it runs its course – and has done so.

So in order to come to terms with your human nature
You have to dig below all the modern sediments
And the humanist sentiments that not only obscure
But falsify the truth, making falsehood appear true.

*

It is rightly said that the truth draws
Its children to itself, pointing the way
To human nature where faith resides
As the true foundation for all that is.

*

So you need to know that your nature is redeemed,
Else why would you choose to make contact with it?
You may take my word for it, that your human nature
Is redeemed, unless you would like to argue
That perhaps your nature is not human at all
But simply a conglomerate of questionable attributes
And you may be right, however I doubt it.
Some have animal spirits and demons
That rule them inside and then outside too,
And recently we have seen some prime examples
That rose to the top of several nations.
Their total absence of human-natural

Attributes allowed them to murder millions
While some were possessed of a little virtue
And only murdered a hundred thousand,
Not to mention the torture that gave them pleasure.
They did this to impose their will
On entire populations, for several years.
Today too one reads about criminals
Who refresh themselves by drawing energy
From children they abuse and from adults they deceive.

You search in your soul for an answer to the question:
How can God allow this to happen?
Or: Why would God allow this to happen?

Even by your question I can tell where you go wrong.
Are you not all at liberty to behave as you would?
Therefore can you not utterly turn away
From merciful spirit and good creativity?
If you break with god, how can god reach you?

I should think that this answers both questions adequately.
If not, you may have to revise what you know
Of god and how you understand his power.
The Mighty God is part modern invention
By caterpillars who refuse to evolve.
Such a god is mighty like his minions are mighty
And he blesses canons on both sides of no-man's-land.
May the best man survive, he says, and smiles.
He enjoys the spectacle – and what is man?

Of course there are also those who prefer
To avoid the challenge of life altogether
And to all intents and purposes they are dead.
The God they invent is bound to be dead,
That goes without saying – and of human nature
There is really not much for them to write home about.

All the same – and this is a teaching I would ask you
To keep well alive in the forefront of your mind:
All are born with potential of redeemed
Human nature which cannot be erased from their being.
However it can be so adamantly ignored
And methodically resisted that they are utterly inhuman.
Their inhumanity may defy description.
However there is always still an increment of humanity,
Which clings to the flesh in which they were born
And remains accessible – god knows how.
If such a man were burnt at the stake
That unaccessed increment would return to the elements.

*

I have not quite finished with human nature yet.
I seem to hear you asking yourself:
Is my human nature redeemed or not?
Evidently you are looking for a sign.
Let me give you a sign, though you may not like it:
When the critical spirit leaves you no peace
And usurps the place of your best interests,
Then you may know that your nature is redeemed.
Fortunate are those who don't need a sign.

*

The other question that still hangs in the air
So far as I can make out from the look on your face
Is: How can I have faith, I, who have no faith?

My first reply to that has to be the following:
If you were brought up to have 'a faith'
And now you have lost it – let's see things as they are –
Count yourself well off, because what you have lost
Was not worth keeping. A faith is not faith.
The one thing that is left for you to do now
Is to contact your human nature within you.

If you don't know how to do even that,
It may be that you haven't suffered enough yet.

Which brings me to the tenth item in my list:
'Creative suffering'; of pain, by the way,
Not histrionics or morbid sentimentality.

*

Let met put it this way: Your redeemed nature,
Which you need to contact to find your faith,
Will not be touched except with clean hands.
So let me ask you the following question:
Do you get emotional when someone mentions
Christ in your presence? Do you feel shame
Or embarrassment when someone mentions Jesus?
To that extent you do not have clean hands.
He is the one who has redeemed your nature.
He did that whether you like it or not,
So my suggestion to you is: Get over it!
It's not the sort of thing you could have done yourself.
So why are you offended, if it's all the same to you?
Be honest with yourself. Stop prevaricating.
I don't say that this present philosophical approach –
Or let's call it the practical application of wisdom –
Is necessarily the appropriate approach for you
If you're looking for a way out of the mess you're in.
However it's a perfectly reasonable way
And if I were you I would give it a try.

*

By pain I mean everything that goes against the grain
Of a human being's existential growth.
The fact that faith has to be involved here
Should not put you off. A lot of what we look at
With a knowing eye seems consequential
When in truth what's involved is simultaneous.

111

Our step by step progress leads to a
Surprise at the end, when it all coincides.

So the fact that you register when your growth is inhibited
Is a good thing, surely, as I've mentioned many times.
The modern mentality doesn't agree with that.
It wants to stay put. Change has to happen
Entirely within some predictable terrain.
Evolution, however, is not at all predictable.
That is precisely how it differs from development.
Development is classic. You fit pieces together
And you end up with something that suits your idea.
So, for example, what has to be matched
Is form and content. The result is to please.
At the same time there is insecurity about the future
Which is taken into account by the mature person.
You develop so that you may eventually evolve.
When the time comes you have your work cut out for you.
What you deal with is *the shape of things to come.*
Shape now prevails. Form diminishes.
And shape needs input, which is called stuff.

Back I turn now to that notion of pain
That will help you to understand creative suffering.
Pain is the stuff that allows shape to prosper.
Pain takes shape due to creative suffering.
Shape is understood in a twofold way.
On one hand it's a work, for others to take advantage,
On the other hand you who do the work overcome
The hindrance that blocks existential growth.

Pain, of course, may be direct or vicarious.
Compassionately you deal with the pain of others.
Your aim will not be to get rid of the pain
But to remove the obstruction to existential growth.

I will say this again because it's ever so important:
Your aim will not be to get rid of the pain
But to remove the obstruction to existential growth.
Those who strive mainly to kill the pain
Only set themselves up for another reminder
Which may end up more intense than the first.
All the same, in this present time, your god has seen fit,
For the sake of those few who shall carry the gift forward,
To shorten the time of the pain rationally
At such times as you decide to call an emergency.
In that case you cause yourself no heavier burden.
Those with the skill will shape their grief,
And certainly, in the case of compassionate transfer,
The pain may always be worked into shape
While words and deeds facilitate improvement.

Whatever the pain, your own or someone else's.
You do well to assume that the pain, in some way,
Will indicate to you how best to proceed
In order to assist evolutionary growth.
When a child weeps, you say: "Where does it hurt?"
If the child cannot say, you trust your intuition
While you continue to love all the more.
How similar to love is this creative suffering!

When first I mentioned the crown of life,
Do you recall what it was that first came to mind?
Yes, compassion. So whether you yourselves hurt,
Or some other being, human or otherwise,
This compassionate love is surely of the essence
Even in the case of creative suffering.

While we are on the subject of creative suffering,
It occurs to me to inform you once again
Of the difference between development and evolution.

I mentioned above that development is classic,
The implication being, that evolution, as eventual,
Is fully expected, hoped for and desired.
The classic work leaves the door open for evolution.
The classic attitude to survival is to see it
As of secondary value, while the primary interest
Is rejection of modernity in the interest of this openness
To evolution as imagined, predicted and anticipated.

Keep in mind that we know modernity as the intention
To avoid evolution at any and all cost
By setting up a system of false values
So that dead-end, everlasting development appears feasible.
Materialism and spiritualism lend themselves to this.
The so-called economy of a modern nation
Must always seem to grow or despair sets in.
This myth referred to as growth is supported
By those who buy for the sake of buying
And eventually a population chokes in its garbage.
So much for the modern materialism.
The modern spiritualism fights its own battles
By coming up with more and more religions
That offer bogus salvation for the price
Of soul exchanged for a permanent psyche.
You can see how modern materialism and spiritualism
Are parallel phenomena, with similar consequences.

I return now to classic development and observe
How those who develop in the hope of evolution
As imagined, predicted and sincerely anticipated,
Often use modernity as a sort of starting-block,
To kick against, as they head in the opposite direction.
They do his by treating it like any other evil:
They cheerfully forgive what they cannot change
And by not resisting it they improve their development.

114

Is there any point in asking: Would you still develop
If modernity did not stare you in the face?
I would advise you never to think about thinking.
It clogs up your mind and causes constipation.

*

The notion of item number ten, creative suffering,
Has borne ample fruit. It only remains to add
That if, during development, you practice this virtue,
It will stand you in good stead as you begin to evolve.

A classically developing human being –
And I have amply shown what I mean by this –
Sees pain principally as a hindrance to his development.
Those who evolve no longer think of pain,
Of misfortune, misery, sickness and unhappiness
As evils but rather – and I have shown this too –
As indicators of present hindrance to growth
And to some extent as pointers in the particular direction
Where this hindrance may successfully be circumnavigated.
Keep in mind what I said about tarrying or following.
These two attitudes to pain then identify
The parameters of the transition from development to evolution.
Actually not much more needs to be made of it.
Hopefully this will help you to count the cost.
It needs to be mentioned that not all are chosen.
Not all see but the one possibility ahead of them
As they set out on their unavoidable resurrection.
Those who choose do well to count the cost,
And having chosen, they need those who are chosen.

*

When you deal with pain, for example with a headache
And a sore throat, once you have set out
On your resurrection, you may confirm yourself

115

As a growing human being, aware of your existence
and able to come up with courage and strength,
also with joy, for you have those within you.
In this way you will expand, in the direction of new life.
While you still developed you asked for joy.
Now that you evolve, you generate joy,
You draw on courage available within you
And you project strength towards the life on its way.

*

Which brings me to item eleven, namely
'merciful love'. You should, by now,
be familiar with love that is no longer possessive.
Jealousy quickly reminds you, something is amiss in your brain.
Now if you play your cards right, you will turn this upside down.

Only those who relish passions as drugs or as poisons
Will toy with this emotion until it self-inflates.
In your youth you wanted to kill the one who caused
Any inflammation of your psyche. Later
You regretted your own susceptibility.

Now, while protecting your self against this passion,
You run the risk of courting contemptuous indifference.
However, consider that in the absence of passions,
passion now can appeal to you as adult feeling.
You value your ability to sense someone else's pain.

At first this may cause you to mingle pain with pity and sentiment.
The one who is in pain may well be shamed by this.
You notice this and wonder how it might be remedied.
Clearly it's up to you to learn how to *suffer creatively*,
Rather than pretending to know what someone's pain is about.

Now you allow yourself to become susceptible to that pain
By caring for that person involved, as though he or she were you.

You are able to discern between the hardship suffered
and that person's actual welfare. In other words
you judge righteously the situation in hand.

The help you offer now may well be slightly different.
First you will seek to suffer that person's pain vicariously
And while this goes on you will wish that person well,
By which I mean that you will love him or her.

Meanwhile you cannot help noticing negative traits.
You may wish to criticise, to give advice on the basis of these,
However the faults you notice are in truth your own
And until you believe this you'd best decide to forego advice.

Instead please love that person, faults and all.
Once you realize that the faults are really your own,
Quickly be grateful that you are able to love that person
mercifully.
One effect this has is your own liberation from those faults.

Thus you are reminded that the one who brought the sword –
I mean the sword that initiated the great development
Against which the modern spirit has since then militated,
Also taught the love that joins the two whole beings.

There are those who assume they love mercifully
If right from the start they practice an indifference
To all that distinguishes one individual
Person from the other, and so they treat all
As though they were tarred with the same brush.

In truth they do not deal with persons at all
But they act as though all were similar individuals,
All to be given the same advice,
The same pre-cooked doctrine of salvation,
Which, in the end, is of no use to anyone

Only persons are susceptible to merciful love,
While individuals insist on their right to be right.
Also be aware that every person is initially bound
To scrape against you in some manner or form.

This is liable to call forth your criticism or disapproval.
You notice this and decide to love that person mercifully.
He or she may well be in need of an evolutionary boost.
The same, at the same time, be assured, is visited upon you.

If you can do this in your own home
You are sure to reap the greatest benefits.
The creation of home, world's microcosm,
Is granted to those who *love mercifully*.

*

Item number twelve is your *'sovereign personality'*
That allows you to act as only you can.
When you live in the world that has no boundaries –
And I hope that by now you have begun to live in that world –
There is no longer any need to wear a mask.
You simply express yourself as you see fit.
What you say, what you do, the silences you choose,
Also most important: what you choose to leave undone,
This originates within your evolving human nature,
Of which you have an image that stands you in good stead.

So now you will probably ask yourself how this
Image of your human nature – in other words
Your human nature as you imagine it –
Can contribute to your communal behaviour.
After all you wish to contribute to your community.
In such a way that both you and it benefit simultaneously.

I reach ahead here a little to the next item which is
Contemporary community but that shall not divert us
From the main theme which is sovereign personality.

Also you will notice that, as usual, I proceed
As spontaneously as possible, so that no thought leads
To the next except by its own inward logic.
In that way the truth is neither side-tracked not impaired.

I return to our theme and begin by pointing out
That you like to think of yourself as individual in every way
Rather than as incorporated in some collective mass.
This certainly shows that your humanity is intact
And not yet – or no longer – driven by an alien force
From which you would have to abstract it
Before you can really think and feel in terms of it.

Being individual, to be fair, you are really like no one else.
I hope that thought does not frighten you. After all
You have come a long way by now from when you still
Compared yourself to others to find out who you were.

Only, if I may make a suggestion:
Try to steer clear of individualism.
Being like no one else is not yet being someone.
So be careful. When you find yourself insisting on being right
You might be a hair's breadth away from spoiling your chances.
Your individual is a plague at every party.
He draws attention to himself and as soon as you heed him
He drops you into some finely fashioned absurdity.
You won't sleep that night, I'll guarantee it.

Above all guard against the individual in yourself.
You see him coming in shallow company,
Then he tugs and pinches and twitches until
Bald-faced lies pop out of your mouth,
Anything for a laugh – but with you at the centre.

I say bury him under a load until he submits.
A load of wise reflection will do the trick.
Your person waits in patience somewhere round he corner,
Where others at the moment seem to be holding her in check.

However that's the old habit of the mask. Not appropriate.
Your person is the one you are to become.
The 'individual' evolves – that's he long and the short of it.

Those near you search you out, ask you questions,
They approach on dove's feet, ever so gently,
Well may you suspect a trick. Stay loose, I say,
But don't necessarily wish them away.
They have a role to play.

As usual, what evolves, first draws itself in,
Too busy at the moment with this and that
To participate in what must seem to it preposterous.
If this is you, suspend your judgement wholly.
A person is not a subdued individual, is not
A student of the pleasing comment, the polite phrase.
Granted, you feel out of it, a stick-in-the-mud, but
Cheer up, you are about to acquire a real face –
Whereupon it will not even take courage to smile.

When first your personality sets sail
You will feel so grateful, so cheerful, so relieved –
Especially because it's not a thing you have achieved
But a being in its own right, without fail.

You will want to dash about, sprint across the lawn,
Dance and caper to your heart's content
Because for once you're in your proper element,
Not by opinions and feelings quartered and drawn.

However I suggest you concentrate on a work
Even while within you good spirit celebrates.
All that ever so pleasant emotion indicates
That your existence has reached the apex of an arc.

True personality likes to involve itself in achievement.
This might be the time to learn a lesson, to hone a skill,
Simply to practice a craft, an exercise of intellect and will.
It matters little what you do, so long as you do it well.

*

This confluence of personality and creativity
May come as a surprise. In company now you like to listen,
To take note of this and that, for later reference,
When what is needed is a kind word or an intimate gesture
To steady a temper or to allay a fear.

Also now arises
Need for affection,
Desire for affection,
Human-natural.

And, as you would expect –
If you were to stand above yourself
Looking down upon your poor mistreated self
The way an astronaut in space looks down on earth,
When down and up no longer make much sense –

You know now what it means to feel
Pain of emotion, and this is drastic.
One moment to be cozened, valued, prized,
Then suddenly cast aside like trash,
No longer wanted among your fellow men.

Little will you know, for some appreciable time,
How this is precisely the call for *sovereign personality*.
When the poor individual, poor thing,
Either slinks off to make room for the new master

Or takes its revenge and kills.
This is the time when the knives come out,
Specifically knives, for some reason, as if cutting
And stabbing and slashing were the order of the day.
The newspapers confess they are gobsmacked.
The politicians realize they're up against it now.

I confess I am much more concerned with *you* now;
And will you no longer 'stand under' but understand?

You are young still, you have entertained hopes,
Will your star really rise, you ask yourself,
Because the opposite, let's face it, is unimaginable,
And what at your age you cannot imagine
Is bound to result in murder and mayhem.

Turn to me then, who is present enough in these lines,
As does he who writes them down for your benefit.
All that you fear to feel has been well suffered through,
There's no need to do it again, fresh from the start.
Here you may inwardly lean towards the one and singular
Role-model supplied by the spirit that has made it
Possible for you to experience panic in the first place.

And pity those, if you must, who cannot for a moment
Entertain the least insecurity, the least uncertainty,
Without shooting up ecstasy. They would enter the kingdom
Through the back door, which just ain't cricket.

*

Sovereign personality. Could you make sense of it?
That which makes you unique is being acted out.
I suggest you step right into the enemy's camp for a moment.
He looks for your individuality, has the knife ready.
Somehow he cannot quite place what is going on within himself.
Perhaps the within-realm has never until now been made
Available for him and he stumbles, inconclusive,
Puzzled by his shadow, the thing his fear casts before him.

It's true that "mankind cannot bear much reality", however
You are being asked, because you can do it, to bear it all.
Believe me, bearing it all is easier than bearing much,
And if this, for you, is a mystery – "let it be".
Would you allow yourself to be used as a tool of wrath?
Let someone else do the dirty work; do you choose
Sovereign personality, merciful love incarnate.

*

At first you will not be all that eager to
Scuttle the clown, to hide the hero away from the
Awe-inspired audience; there are some bad habits
That take time to melt before the ethical awareness.
Do not, I say, do not even pretend, to play a role,
I mean the role of the lackadaisical, the devil-may-care
Social adjunct, who hides his feelings, his thoughts.
In other words, don't try to be popular. It won't suit you;
Not since you're still sitting here reading this.
People themselves have that market cornered
And they're good at it, don't try to compete.
You won't, in the end, respect yourself
And neither will anyone else.

It's all the same whether you're picked or chosen,
Admit it, you're standing outside, you're frozen.

The next attempt you make to join a club
Will be your next disappointment. That's the rub.
Stand on your two feet, feel that delicious gravity.
You are the only one standing here. Don't snub

Those who stand elsewhere. Or maybe they fly,
Because gravity is something they just don't swear by.
For you – earth below, blue sky above, the stars at night
And always the next good work in sight.

*

Sovereign personality, the sweetest fruit on the tree of life!
Here is something you can get your teeth into.
You work your way forward from one insult to the next,
Trading punches with your own ego if necessary;
Calculating the odds when you're down and out.

Does it sound as if I meant that you should
Say and do whatever you like? God forbid!
A sovereign personality presupposes a sovereign person.
These are not merely terms descriptive of processes.
I wish I could rely on you to be patient with your judgment.

A person, strictly speaking, is itself a spiritual achievement.
You do not become a person except by weighing consequences.
Let thinking and doing be known to be right at times,
At other times truthful, useful, loving and merciful.
And shall you not school yourself from one lesson to the next?

Certainly there must be exposure to world,
To society and community. What if the one next to you
Attacks your right to exist? Or the State challenges your honesty?
Or what you consider to be apt flies back in your face?
There will be some hitches and you will be glad you've escaped,
But this is how you as a person are formed and then shaped –
Given your upright spirit, strength of character and clean hands.

Sovereign in the sense that you do as you see fit
And if they pull you up for it you overlook it.
Sovereign because you crave justice – not for yourself
But for those whose very existence hinges upon justice
But they cannot speak up for themselves.
Sovereign beyond contention, beyond the categories
That cut off the day to day circulation.

I'd like you to sit still for a moment to consider
How much you might have to gain from prayer,
Because actually, now that I think of it, this is where
Your sovereign personality takes shape,
Between you and good spirit, both in person.
No, but draw breath, hang about while I
Develop my theme, for your eyes only.

We are gradually working our way around to
Our next item, contemporary community, and for that
You need to be au fait with respect to what goes on
When creature and creator meet face to face.
I entrust you with one of my favourite concepts: pattern.
Here, in prayer, which, by the way, you can do all the time,
You may observe exemplary exchanges of
Human/divine substance – I mean humanity.

The creator spirit, as you may as well know –
And I speak here from intimate familiarity and insight –
Will search you out for what is best in you
And exchange for it, from his own, what is good.
There now you have what we all mean by communication.
Prayer as the practice-ground for communication,
I cannot make it simpler. Again and again
We meet and greet, exchange pleasantries and then
Something happens – oh lord! If only you knew!

What am I saying! Surely you soon will.
I am not confiding in you so that at the next trivial opportunity
You will spill half digested mysteries in the street.
Pray and know that what you do is
Classic development towards endless evolution.
You are schooling your sovereignty at the university of love.
All I can do here is put you in the right mood,
The rest is up to you. Talk it over with your friends.

*

This is where our discussion of the sovereign personality ends
And I invite you to take the next logical step in this venture –
Which is also a quest, as you may have noticed.
'*Contemporary community*' is item thirteen.

It is not only natural but human-natural, that upon a
Sufficiency of prayer (I mean prayer that leads into work
And really amounts to work in its own right) you will wish to
Reach out to your fellow human being, to let him or her
Know that you exist, that you have some life to give,
Life that you would like to share – if that were possible
And if some way to achieve that could be found.
I must tell you in all honesty and sincere care for you welfare
That this sort of approach is usually most expedient.

Yes, I know that in your weakness you fear rejection
And in your ego you will either be sure to get it,
Which will serve you right, in the best sense of 'serve',
Or worse, you will take up with another ego
And there goes your precious life out the window,
Where it blows upon an elemental wind. So –
In order to avoid all such eventualities, prepare
Within yourself the kind of approach I have suggested.
You invite a guest not only into you house but into your home.

I intend to explain both elements that combine
To make what I have called contemporary community.

Community, of course, depends upon communication
And I have made a start by letting you know
How I would initially go about it if I were you.
Speaking of my being you, as you no doubt read between the lines,
This is not a notion so far fetched as you may think.
The writer of these lines does his best to communicate my wishes,
Because he is of the persuasion that I have what it takes
To supply you with what is both essentially and existentially
good for you. I suggest we all try to appreciate
our common bond of human-natural affection,
which is rare enough these days.

Communication by means of sovereign personality
Is what I mean, to be sure, and when I add
'contemporary' to that equation I am not adding much.
All the same, try to keep in the forefront of your mind
And not in the back, from where so much leaks out these days,
That contemporary also means 'not modern'.
'Modern', you will recall, implies rejection of human evolution.
'Contemporary', therefore, suggests its acceptance.
Even that much of a comparison shows some gold.

I myself suggest that when you set out to communicate
you do your best always to keep a beady eye out for
what can be learned now that cannot be learned in any other way.
Communication, you see, especially if prepared by
Habitual good prayer, (the aim of prayer is similar)
Is always to deliver you, somewhat, in the direction of
Hale, hearty and whole human being. At this stage
I do not essentially distinguish between a comment to someone
At the bus stop and a communicable work like the present.

I recall your awareness of the sword brought by the one
Who separated massive antiquity into manageable halves.
He did this; I'm sorry, it's a fact. And it's done, so
I suggest you make your peace with it. In that particular light,
Communication is a case of managing those halves.
They arrive on your doorstep in a million and a half guises
So that you may take your pick and do a job of sorts.
You sort out some half so that you may present it
To someone who is willing to come up with the other, sorted, half.

I realize I am taking you into the thick of it here.
I am asking the writer to hone his language a bit.
Contemporary also means present in the light of day.
Never try to communicate while your mind is on something else.
Are you wanting to instruct some youngster in the integral calculus?
Don't forget to communicate. Are you about to participate in the
Performance of a Schumann Konzertstück for a select audience?
Don't forget to communicate. Your baby child will not
Accept the breast? Are you remembering to communicate?

You see what I mean, don't you. Communication is really
An additional impulse most of the time in your day,
Most necessary because of your wilful intellect and your
Intellectual will – pardon me for getting into that.
The modern spirit has devised so many modes of
Non-communication – fiendishly clever, so many of them –
That contemporary communication is liable to occur to you
As somewhat exotic or as an extravagance.
Please, it's the most human-natural engagement in the world.

Alas, the modern spirit will be with you for a while, waiting
To pounce, critically, as soon as you neglect your resurrection.
I have to tell you this in confidence now,
That the critical spirit, the one who undermines your confidence

And shames you in public and tempts you in private,
In short who tries to keep you separated into public and private halves,
Is the only real sign you have that *contemporary community*
Is making inroads upon your otherwise sluggish corporeality.
Contemporary community, in that sense, is therefore
An aspect of the new and live reality pressing in upon you,
Even to the point that at times you wish you were rid of
The very sign that let's you know that it does so.

The modern spirit is critical. It is the sign of the crisis.
What crisis? The new reality is on its way.
It wants you to communicate. It presses you
To ignore all those reason you come up with for
Rejecting one another, commonly on account of
Alleged misdemeanours in the past, and instead
Making room for one another within yourselves,
As I indicated above. It's the sort of activity that
Goes against the grain at first – the bad grain.

Contemporary communication goes against the grain
Of your collective corporeality. Now there's a mouthful.
I would like you to learn to identify this horrible feeling
Rather than trying to get rid of it as soon as possible
By fair means or foul. Identify it correctly as what it is.
Know what it amounts to, understand what it means.
It amounts to an interruption of the presence of good spirit.
What it means is an increase in good spirit for you.
You are capable of knowledge and understanding, so therefore
Be ready to apply these sharply at short notice.

I see your curiosity is aroused. What I suggest is
That the crisis you know dissolves. This first:
Identification of the modern crisis,
Critical spirit clamouring for attention.

You are to know it simply for what it is, namely
The modern, critical spirit, ready to be known.
Has it paralyzed your faculty of knowing?
Have you with lightning speed reacted,
with murderous hatred – so how can you know now?

Don't be annoyed with me, please, for taking you through this
Seeming series of impossibilities, narrowed down
To become quickly manageable with feather-light touch;
Fiendish injustice every time, such obvious idiocies,
If only there were someone who would agree with you
That this is intolerable, too much to ask, pure evil!
And now you are not even allowed the bitter retort!
No one to praise you for flattening this most insidious enemy!
You know him so well, superfluously reacquainted
Time and again as if to rub something in –

A truth perhaps? Yes, of course. It has to be reiterated,
To be restated, time and again, in this way and that way.
If only there were more of you who would agree to
Put it in their own manner and mode, courageously!
Like a tricky passage for piano, for violin:
First study what it means in itself, within context,
Then work out the fingering, with gentle deliberation
Repeating the movement – it only seems endless –
Until you have it by heart – or outwardly, 'auswendig'.
Out here in the light of day we need inwardly canny warriors
Against this inside, insidious, seeming mixer of poisons.

So this is my reason for turning and returning to that same
Knowing of the soul-pain, yes, the soul-pain, that
Knocks you for six, pretends to persuade you to make
Sweeping judgements, to inflict punishments,
'écrasez l'infâme', 'die Endlösung', that sort of thing,
You experience it in your own breast: 'Never again!'

This is how the critical spirit makes itself felt
As the psyche of the unprepared, the emotionally immature –
In the very flesh of the coward and the critic.

It may help you, when you look around and you see
So many people happy and content; it wouldn't
Occur to them even to wonder what you might mean
By pain of the soul. They look at you and they say:
You must be ill, you better look for professional treatment.
Your doctor will identify disorders and syndromes
And then he will proscribe and prescribe.
No use mentioning soul; he only knows psyche,
While yours is not lost to you yet.

Enough said, many look happy without a soul,
So you must not let them shame you when they look at you
As though you were from another planet. However
React often enough to critical spirit
And your psyche will come along nicely
Until one day you stab your friend – or even a stranger
Who had looked at you in a way that set off an explosion.
So get into the habit of knowing the danger ahead of time
And understand what it means to be tested by the modern spirit.

Come to think of it, I have not explained that yet;
At least not in the present context. What I mean is
The plain and simple insight, at a moment's notice,
Into the predicament of the one through whom this spirit
Comes into the world. – He or she is worthy of compassion.
"Evil must come into the world but woe onto him – " etc.
Here is someone now who is trying to kill your soul,
This is certainly what it feels like to you,
However he or she is in a position of authority
And evidently believes he or she is doing you some good.

If you become what would be called disrespectful,
Perhaps by showing your annoyance or expressing disgust,
This would amount to a reaction to the modern spirit

And believe it or not, it would harm your soul,
Even though for a moment it might make you feel better.
Dumb insolence from you would have the same sad effect.
If you were to understand now that this individual is
In the grip of this nihilistic spirit, do you suppose you might
Be able to come up with some compassion from him or her?

Compassion, by the way, is the soul strengthener.
Modernity, by comparison, is the psyche fortifier.
Now which do you suppose is more powerful in the end:
Criticism or compassion? Corporality or communality?
The following is also well worth thinking about:
The power of compassion builds *contemporary community.*
By the power of compassion, you in person, each and
Every time, build and give shape to contemporary community.
You find yourself here at the centre of beautiful action.

In the presence of soul psyche is healed. This too
Must often be repeated. Psyche is soul in denial.
What has your soul, that it might cling to, for security,
In the face of the modern, massive emphasis?
Shall I come right out with it or must I fear
A reaction from you, ashamed as you are
Of your distance from the truth in person, or offended
By the one whose speech betimes reaches you
In your private silences? How shall I know what is best?

At the very heart of contemporary community
You may imagine every single individual person's freedom
To contribute what only he of she can bring to the fore
In aid, so that a few, several or many are helped
In their ongoing search for life and appreciation of life.
Think of this community as an outpouring of strength
From your heart, mind and soul, and know that it grows
And that it tends to grow, reminding you of this at times
When you close yourself off from your fellow man.

Take for example the one who accuses his fellow man
Of a misdemeanour and he has not looked into his own heart.
Who can say: 'You are a racist!' without being a racist?
Or who can say: 'You are anti-Semitic, sexist, chauvinist!' or
What all the labels are moderns hang around one another's necks,
Without him- or herself being that very thing at that moment?
Do but extend your contemporary communal spirit and
Notice how these paper tigers collapse into themselves.
Inevitably they roar just a little before they burst into flames.

*

I have said all I want to say at the moment about
Contemporary community and turn my attention to
The fourteenth item, which is the 'light of day', in which we
Show who we are and what we are made of. This is
Not the same as what I mean by daylight, for it encompasses
Our active and passive being, both without and within.
What I mean by daylight helps me to differentiate
The fullness of my being here and now from what appears
To the eyes of all, however they are composed or disposed.

I wonder has it occurred to you how much it matters
What your next move is? You suppose you behave in
This or that way, and somehow your behaviour is bound to
Fit into the pattern of general behaviour as perceived
By no one in particular and is therefore inconsequential.
In reality the opposite is true. Every move you make
Either helps or hinders. Did you suppose you were of
No account? Allow me to remind you that this is not so.
You are here on the earth today to some particular good end.

In the light of day, not in some back alley or cooped up
In your study; not in front of an audience or while
Out for a stroll in the sunshine where the wheat fields
Shimmer in the distance and a brook babbles nearby –
Or rather anywhere at all may you know your destiny,

133

As long as you search in the *light of day*, not elsewhere.
Can you not recall that time when you stood much in the sun
But were always in darkness? And if that word 'destiny'
Does not jar too much on your nerves I offer it to depict
The true and purposeful reason for your being around.

Why are you around in the *light of day* in the first place?
Let that be your destiny. However, that is another story.
I cannot imagine why you would balk at the suggestion
That a concept is required to point you to where you may
Contact in some meaningful manner, at that particular time,
The definition of your next step forward – or call it
The limits and bounds of how next to proceed in the interest
Of the good, the true an the beautiful. Where shall you
Search for this meaning? – Leisurely in the light of day.

Yes, quite right, leisure is appropriate in the light of day,
Where you search for meaning appropriate to your
Present stage of existence in growth. Without leisure
You run into difficulties here – which is strange
Because you so readily associate excellence with effort.
Ask a contemporary painter. He will tell you: The brush
Knows as well as I do, and sometimes even better,
Where to go next. Or the speaker who finds himself
In some contemporary setting, I mean where
The pressure builds and ignorance holds sway:

'Let yourself float, in leisurely fashion, in the light of day,
Almost as if in the moment the truth were alert to inform
Your heart and head, your brain and flesh, of the next
Proposition appropriate to impart, though it may seem
That the seam between now and then must surely be
All too obvious – but then just because you yourself have not
Annealed the joint, after a time in the heat, after hammer and tong,
That does not mean that the truth has not settled precisely
There, and look, they understand perfectly well, before me.

So I inform you that all the so-called arts have to find
Their contemporary meaning in the *light of day*, and at leisure.
He who still finds that he prides himself for the genius
In his flesh, look, he must fail. The modern criticism
Will no longer support him, and a good thing too, because
What is on the cards now has to hold water and be fire-proof.
For that, brothers and sisters, you need the help of the
Meek and mild one, so that together the communal truth
Shall marry the communal beauty and the twain be real.

There's a new excitement in the air that needs to be
Incorporated, not flaunted. Engaged with, not wasted.
It annihilates some of the efforts you have been
known to make, you were praised for them, labours
that gained you recognition in high and low places.
Now you flail about, mayhap in a panic in deep water,
And if you're not careful you will try to pass off these
Cries for help as though they amounted to monuments
When in fact you might have waited patiently for help.

The performer of music will have to dig deep both
Into himself and into the score to find light-of-day-
Enlightenment that veritably desires to seep into
His fingers, his vocal chords, his limbs and his stance.
Nothing new about that, you may say, however musicians
Have always been in the forefront of the arts and
They before others have arrived at the conclusion that
They communicate not for the money, via will and intellect,
But their invisible body has to be laid on the line.

Another thought I want to pass on to you in relation to
The *light of day* is that here, as nowhere else, human
Relations are readily sponsored in a fashion that makes
Reward and punishment superfluous from the start.
Art, as the means of informing and reminding you of
Your human nature, helping you to catch up if you have
Lost track, that sort of thing, and not necessarily as an

135

Introduction to extreme feelings, extraordinary sentiments
And the like, requires a space about which we can all agree.

This is a space in which artists as such feel lost. I'm afraid
I have to tell you this to steer you away from something
That embarrasses you because you cannot understand it.
No one, least of all the artists, understands the artist, so
Why should you? I have decided on a spot of redefinition.
The artist does not do what he does in the light of day
But in some dark corner, where he anxiously steers a line
Between the modern crisis and magic. Oh dear, I suppose
I will, eventually, have to explain what I mean by those two.

At the moment suffice it to say that the choice of the *light of day*
Is not the artist's light, by and large on account of the lack of
Magic and a crisis between which he must steer his course.
In the light of day, as you may know, what rules the roost is
The spirit of truth, a most peaceful fellow and charming –
Charming in the sense of congenial, cordial and gracious –
Who is willing to enlighten you by means of this light, avoiding
The idea of the supernatural and vicarious indulgence in death.
Oh dear, what does that leave to put bums in seats, you say?

What you need to find is someone who is willing to go
Beyond the modern parameters of magic and criticism.
Actually it will seem more like a case of relaxing *out* of it
And letting the truth in the light of day speak for itself.
Distinct imagination will delight especially in this move,
For now it is able to evolve without disturbing thought –
Which often turns into a nightmare for the modern artist,
Who cannot imagine and think at one and the same time.
That is why I leave him now as I turn to the art-worker.

In the light of day the art-worker is perfectly at home.
He will not allow himself to be sidetracked by questions
Such as: 'Why am I doing this?' or 'Will my work be accepted?'

Simply because he could not do otherwise. There is
Nothing he could do differently. His world is circumscribed
By talent or gift and genius in such a way that whatever
Announces itself to him as experience, that is his life,
And thereafter, from out of himself in combination with
What he knows and understands he says what he says.

It makes no sense to say that the art worker is not free to
Speak as he wishes, since whatever he wishes he can say
And all that pertains to his work exists in the light of day.
He differentiates, therefore, between the light of day in which
He works and the daylight in which he exists and grows.
What he takes from one realm to the other is simply
His personal knowledge of himself as a human being like
Other human beings who are affected by 'the time of day'
Like himself, but who know nothing of the *light of day* –
Except through his works. Here he initiates them into
Human nature as it is when whole and complete, not
Fragmented, remote, unpredictable and incalculable.
You may understand therefore that his work has meaning
For those who value their human nature and who regret
Its shortcomings, aberrations, weaknesses and distortions
For which they themselves feel responsible in the sense
That they see it as their god-given task to complete it.
They will know the light of day, not magic and criticism.

Magic is modern man's substitute religion. He sincerely
Wishes he could live in 'the land of magic' and he
Surrounds his children with plenty of magical artefacts
So as to give them a good grounding in it – before the
Unavoidable 'horrors' of daylight begin to take their toll.
I don't want to come across as a spoilsport, but you know,
It's not even a beginning for them, a foretaste of bliss,
But a drug, a high, an adrenalin kick, then tedium again.
This is not the place for analyzing the physiology of magic.

137

As for criticism, you know by now that this is the one
Sign we have of the approaching final reality, the kingdom
Not of the earth. Certainly the entrance of the truth in person
Into the world constituted a crisis right from the start;
and for every 'individual' – as we are bound to call him – this
Crisis is liable to appear on his horizon. Is he prepared?
Or does he himself now become a critical individual who
Exists all his life in crisis, in other words, does he embrace
Modernity with all its defensive misfortunes and crises?

Magic is the sun that peeps through the chinks in the wall
Of the modern prison cell. For two millennia modernity
Has been the predicament of those who rejected the classic
Development towards evolution and instead insisted on
Magic and criticism, which shuts the door to evolution.
Modern man forever discovers and invents, outside of himself,
Defensive and provocative substitutes for what he might
Come upon within himself if … well, if he were otherwise.
You are not to argue with him. He has his critical role to play.

The purpose of works like the present is to help those who
Wish to come into the light of day – who desire the realization
Of their highest hopes in spite of their worst fears and who
Will not rest until they have carved out a niche for themselves
In the 'kingdom of heaven on earth', from where they may serve
that same purpose, not fighting evil but doing good. However
The struggle with the modern dilemma cleanses and frees them.
Always the spirit of truth is willing to abide with them, even
As they are willing to abide in it, endlessly patient with change.

* * *

I have taken you to the top and you have stayed with me.
Now I will ask you to gather all your resources
Because the descend down the other side of this mountain
Will not resemble the way a skier slaloms down a snow slope
Or the way a base jumper leaps off the edge and glides down.

Instead you will have to conquer every foot of distance carefully
Because an accident would end in injury and perhaps death.
I realize that this must sound preposterous when applied
To a work such as the present, however this is not entertainment
But a rational way forward into mature human behaviour.

From the outset therefore, as you begin your descent into
Regions of more communal relevance to your growth,
I should like you to keep in mind that you are not on your own
But in the company of someone who has been on this journey
Many times, and always with a person like yourself,

Who was interested in the ways and means whereby he might
Aid and abet the establishment of this great kingdom which
Transcends in its purpose all that exists and is imaginable,
Primarily on the earth, where every little thing must come true,
But also in the minds and hearts of men, women and children.

*

You surely understand by now that you cannot come down from
This height of many insights and experiences unless first
You look back upon your progress up to this point in order to
Evaluate what you have achieved, even if you cannot altogether
Encompass it in the same light, which is understandable.

So you might liken the existential spiral to a specifically human
Growth pattern that illustrates how human beings initially
Flee from their destiny out of fear of being falsified, for they
Picture their truth as somehow related to their individuality.
Consequently the truth in person cannot occur to them.

No wonder, therefore, that I showed you right away how to
Instigate and design a kind of flight-pattern, which would
Allow you to soar supreme, out of reach of your ingrained
Bad habits, such as that cowardly association with the
Like-minded and the feverish multiplication of attachments –

139

Called adultery. In fact each time you made such a wrong move
I cut you off. Sometimes you despaired but most often you
Rose to the occasion, conquered your falsehood and turned
Courageously to where you imagined I must be hiding.
To that end then I always concealed myself wisely.

Now however you are no longer a stranger to those parts
Where life has eventually rooted. Let those be the safe-houses
Where you seek shelter when the elements behave catastrophically
Or when you are at risk of losing your balance. This happens
When you descend too rapidly into a whirlpool of emotion.

I would also caution you that sometimes, when you seek my
Advice and assistance, it is important for your welfare that I
'Appear to be absent'; that where you have encountered me
in the past there is empty space – for you to step into and fill.
Each time be sure to expect a moment of despair or anger.

As you take your first few steps downward from the peak
You notice in the distance, projected onto mists from below,
A phantom of an image, depicting, as it were, many people
In distress, as though unable to decide for themselves
Whether they should move or stand still, speak or remain silent.

For a moment you cannot decide whether anything is
Expected of you, so you hesitate and observe these gestures
Of uncertainty; then you decide to take a closer look and
As you step forward you realize that yet another step
Would have taken you over the edge to your death.

What came over you and rescued you as it brought you
To your senses was an inward rush of intense heat.
You reflect on this and consider quite rightly that
In future you will do well to guard sober presence of mind,
While at the same time you do not neglect to be grateful.

You would be right to assume that it was I who prevented
Your downfall and that it was not I who produced that
Mirage-like illusion. If you now contemplate these two
Facts side by side you will have in your hands a tool
Most useful for you in future for the purpose of learning.

I recall to your mind that you evolve. You have behind you
The classic development which required a type of learning,
However now you learn to learn what is required for the
Purpose of 'bearing fruit'. Much of consequence then
Concurs now and you are forgiven in advance for a

Multitude of errors of misjudgement you are bound to make
As time and again you discover this simultaneity where
Previously you depended upon causal relationship to
Guide you through mental processes. In physical,
Endless world all happens and is done here and now.

I mention this in passing. Do not expect to be able to
Make any lasting sense of it now. When you evolve
You are always in cooperation with me and I am
Ready to steer you in the right direction as soon as you
Ask for this. If you do not ask, things may get a bit painful.

Mind you, your asking has to be of the most intimate.
Some think by pushing words in my direction and then
Waiting in vain for a response, this means I am not.
I am that I am and nothing you can do will stop me from
Being, since being after all is what it is as I.

So ask yourself, even before you make some effort to
Impress yourself upon me or the world, whether or not
You are. This is a sensible question. What is the point of
Wondering are you worthy, are you loved, are you
Here on the earth for a reason today – if you are not?

Right away then I consider that you might like to learn
How to be – just in case, upon careful checking, you decide
That no, indeed, you are not and good gracious, what now!
Turn to me therefore right away. If you are in any doubt
About where to find me, does this upset you at all?

If it does not, then you'd best wait a while, until the
Full meaning of your condition is impressed upon you.
It will occur to you as a measure of unease. Immediately
You may know that I am a function of that unease, so
Suffer it gladly and with no further ado here I am.

So it may be important for you to learn that being is
The evolutionary concomitant of developmental faith,
And that the sure way to fail to be is to insist that you are.
You may take account of the full tragedy of it when you see
How a modern individual maintains forcefully that he is.

Why else would we be on this journey together
If I by myself had no care for human beings and if you,
Equally by yourself, were able to be nothing but a
Total failure? Do please consider the implication of that.
Only by virtue of being together can we be who we are.

Now you must not, as I have often reminded, allow yourself
To be confused or to become hateful in the company of
Those who have made of me an idol, who have lifted me
Out of themselves unto a plinth or to the top of a mountain
Or who continue to build houses for me to be happy in.

This is their way of avoiding me a little longer and can you
Blame them when you realize that in order to accept me
They would have to forego what is most precious to them,
Which is all their own special notions of themselves,
Such as that they are perfectly alright as sensitive robots.

I am not surprised that you feel cold all over when you
Hear me say this right out loud as if no one were listening.
The very second you stop reading this, you will probably
Enter an entirely different world, where none of this holds,
But if it holds in you, you have nothing to worry about.

I know full well that there are those who maintain that I
Do not exist. This is hardly surprising, since they themselves,
As I have shown in the previous section on development,
Refuse to exist, unwilling to grow as they are, consequently
Unable to see the world and themselves as other than divorced.

However we shall continue with our careful descent.
You will notice that the air has cleared now and that you
Feel like scampering ahead without a care in the world,
So in order to protect you against mishap I shall allow you
To feel a cramp in your leg, not very serious, just enough

To make you reflect a little. I know it will not take much
Because you have accustomed yourself to understanding
Pain as a benevolent reminder. Thank you, I am so glad,
Because believe me, I take no delight in causing pain.
It is always a case of a little so as to stave off a lot.

Now that you are in perfect moral and ethical balance again
I draw your attention to the young woman, almost a girl still,
Just to the left of that dolerite outcrop there, where the ice
Has evidently caused her to trip and you can see by the way she
Massages her ankle and her foot that all is not well with her.

You look at me as if you wanted me to tell you what to do.
That, however, I must leave to you. I am not your conscience.
Of course I am glad to stand by and comment while you
Continue with what you are doing now, which is admirable.
You are asking her, does she need assistance and she says yes.

143

It's a simple enough request and readily granted, however for the
Sake of our work in hand why not turn it into a case in point,
To illustrate a few side-issues. You are only beginning to evolve
And much still depends on how you interpret your sensations.
Your priority will not be what you stand to gain for yourself here.

Nothing is quite so subtle as a human being's gender affection.
Oh, if you were half dead, there would be nothing to worry about,
However, due to your upbringing, you have been with me
Throughout your youth and are therefore full of the life that
Comes with youth, which is felt and always in need of expression.

Or at least so it seems. However this is an important illusion
Because it brings to your attention as nothing else could
That the way you behave now can be moral or ethical.
If moral, your primary care will be to do nothing wrong and
Because you are young you will succeed only partially.

Why is this so? I wish I did not have to go into such detail,
However if it stops you from rushing off into destruction
At a time when instead useful construction is possible,
I do not hesitate to play the benign philosopher. Morality,
To be blunt, is of no use to you at this time of your life.

While we keep the alternative in mind, allow me to point out
How wrong it would be to cause you to diminish your joy,
To brake you energetic behaviour, for no other reason
than that you might do yourself or someone else harm.
Instead allow me to make you aware of myself.

Allow me to put it this way: There are high spirits heedless
Of harm and high spirits heedless of me. Both involve risk,
Since high spirits are heedless, however morality clings
To misfortune to be avoided, while what you need at
Your age of approaching manhood is an image of fortune.

So this is the time when I try my best to open your eyes –
In the only way that this can be done – to myself
And to the vast possibilities of real, not imaginary life,
That reside within you where I have planted them prior to
Your birth, yes, innately, where I alone have the care of them.

Is it any wonder that so many prophets and priests go astray
Who insist that they alone, with their magic and sorcery,
Have what it takes to put you in touch with me and my benefits,
When in truth all they can do is raise the consciousness of
Need and dread, of want and scarcity – and finally

Of themselves as supposedly indispensible guardians and
Teachers. So once again: Consciousness is not awareness.
Consciousness of me makes me out to be massive and mighty,
Which is old and predates my revelation of myself as
Human, paternal, childlike in wisdom and merciful.

The fact that I have raised humanity to a higher level
Is difficult for most and they prefer might and terror of might,
Allegedly to keep them, mostly others, in line, and thereby
To shut me out, so that they may be modern and mighty.
Therefore I propose to you the possession of childlike awareness.

A spiritual motivation, a spiritual awakening, both are required,
Before you will take it upon yourself gradually to practice
Ethical awareness: doing good to others rather than
Guarding them against harm, which is of secondary importance.
Besides, harm looks quite different in that light.

                              *

When I say that I myself have to alert you to my presence,
I am saying something that not many will be glad to hear
Because they pride themselves on converting others to the faith,
And of course the faith they mean is not faith in me
But faith in systematic dogma, arrived at politically.

145

What I tell you here now is, and will end up being, personal truth,
As all truth is personal, revealed to one person; not opinion,
Because opinion is never of the truth but of things and the
World of things. How a reader approaches this revealed truth,
And what he does with it, has to be entirely up to him or her.

All that can convert someone to faith – not *the* faith – is
Each and every time personal example, behind which I stand.
If I am not present, nothing will come of it. When I am present
I am present personally in and through a human being
And never vicariously through what is made or manufactured.

However let us keep in mind that a human being is
Such a being as knows and understands me by faith and reason.
So much comes together here that has to be taken for granted.
The massive and mighty God has a popular voice and is modern.
Look, he has nearly mopped up what they call their Religion.

*

So not any faith, to which you are persuaded, but I alone
Can move you to know and understand me, to which end
Faith within you, perhaps for the fist time, is ignited
As the spiritual foundation for your physical being on earth.
Any faith of which you are conscious is right away removed.

So now you have this awareness within you with which
You learn to cope. Your resurrection is now underway.
You look around you and many of those you have known
You know no longer. You have a sense of real life now
Of which they have none. To you they must seem dead.

It can take a while to come to terms with that. You are separated
From parents, relations and friends while you learn this new
Mode of behaviour, this new way of being and doing and
Who can say how long this takes, for each of you has a
Different background, a different character. Also your nature

146

Is unique and there is not another on earth just like you.
When you meet another of my children you will know this,
However this does not mean that you will greet and share
Your experiences and compare notes on your resurrection.
You may well do so, but you would do well not to expect it.

I am speaking of the time at the beginning of your resurrection,
When you come to the conclusion, gradually, secretly,
That indeed you are one of the anointed, one of the chosen few
Who have what it takes to usher in my original reality
And to bring it to fruition, first within yourself and then

For others who are able to accept what you are able to give.
Now please try to imagine first how this is something that
Goes on forever and that no final state is to be expected,
When all the apples, so to speak, are in the basket for taking
To market. Eternal life on earth goes on forever and ever.

I should like you all, my children, to present this good news
In your own way, so that each learns to present his or her
Own beauty and truth, for acceptance by those who can accept.
And the good news is that I am among you as *human being*
And as the one who shares in all your trials and tribulations.

This one, whose name I dare not mention since so much
That is wrong and unhelpful has been said about him,
Is with you in spirit and in reality, showing the way to each
And taking upon him much of the hardship that would perhaps
Discourage you utterly, however keep in mind that pain

Itself leads the way for you, in that it shows you where the
Shoe pinches, so that you may deal with it. The true path
Is not the one that leads to a final supernatural happiness
But the one that is itself real life and living reality, so forget
This Shangri-La at the end and help to realize the here and now.

And please make no attempt to flee from the here and now
Except perhaps for short periods when you feel that
Too much is being expected of you, however view this as an
Emergency and not as a permanent state of seclusion from
what is loosely called ordinary existence in the light of day.

If I see fit to abstract you for a time from your fellow man,
This will be plain to you and you will not misunderstand it
As a call to a monastic existence where you would decompose
To such an extent that you would no longer be able to respond
To the everyday experience of those you are here to nourish.

No, by all means hide your true nature until you are more
Familiar with it, while you respect, rather than fleeing from,
Those who will not know your truth, not now, perhaps later.
Reject not a one, for it quite suffices that they reject me.
Count it good fortune that this is entirely my own business.

Your business, at this early stage of your evolution, is
To concern yourself with meaning and purpose of what wells
Up within you and demands attention. No one will
Draw from you explanations of why you are as you are.
Either they quietly know or else they do not wish to know.

As for the young woman or girl who needs assistance
There, only a short distance down from the peak,
Be assured what she needs is generic affection, quite
Independently of what she says she wants or needs.
Thus you can readily assist her, without trepidation.

The other gender does not, perhaps, readily appeal to you
In a way that corresponds with popular expectations,
But why would you draw conclusions from that? Simply
Be and do as you see fit. People delight in name-calling.
You look for recognition within yourself, where I am.

Perhaps you feel you ought to throw yourself into some
Particular activity; you have more energy than you
Know what to do with. Do it well and know it as
Preliminary business, as what you also do, rather than
Turning it into your life's career, which is deadening.

Or, perhaps most of all, you would like to sit still and reflect.
As soon as possible learn how to pretend that
All is well with you and they will leave you alone.
Your inner light provokes them. Put them at their ease.
Not you but they are to be pitied, if pity must be exercised.

In the end, know that a little persecution does you good.
It draws you out of yourself, persuades you to take a good look
At your priorities. Perhaps you are bit silly, a bit stupid,
Which could readily be rectified, not by making more of an
Effort, as they suppose, but by doing something creative.

Being creative! – We have arrived where a slender, lengthy
Waterfall snakes down along the face of that cliff and the
Spray shimmers in all colours while the sun shines.
Suddenly a wayward description of this phenomenon
Occurs to you and you experience a moment of rest.

Such rest from striving is not to be scoffed at, because
During the time of it something is placed within you
Handy for reference and I call it an illness healed. You are
Barely out of your teens, how can there be talk of illness?
While you abide in me you are well, when you stray you are ill.

And you do stray, oh yes, continuously and repeatedly,
Unless you are most particularly blessed; then only
Now and again, however nonetheless. During your resurrection
You often gain as much from straying as from abiding,
You might as well take this on board, it will help you.

So what I have given you here is a redefinition of illness
And look, it appears in a positive light, like everything
That occurs to you or burdens you or enlivens you
During the rest of your existence on earth now as your
Resurrection proceeds and you harvest the sun's light.

Time and again you will notice that an illness has been healed.
Get to know, as soon as you can, the important difference
Between wellbeing and illbeing. The latter, as you may guess,
Is like the seedbed of the former. The abstraction of yourself
From among the dead is a wonderful exercise of diminution.

Yes, you make little of it. In its smallness an illness can be
Beautiful but only inasmuch as it leads you to renewal of
Wellness. You will hardly need to be reminded that
Dwelling on illness is an outright curse for which you yourself
Might be responsible, but not always. There is that system.

I mean, of course, yet again, that modern system of relegating
All that is truthful and life-furthering to a secondary position:
The survival of the fittest, when fitness means superlative
Adherence to critical values and survival means prolongation
Of lifelessness, postponement and delay of the grave.

Even the language you speak, as you notice, is resurrected.
So as soon as you dwell on an illness, studying it, analyzing it,
Taking delight in talking about it at all, to friends and foes,
You play into the hands of those who prefer survival to life.
Here you have come upon what I will call the caution of a lifetime.

Not that some great creators in the past have not noted this
Peculiar correspondence of illness with creativity, how the
Tiniest of visions will suddenly call forth a quick recognition
Of wellness to be gained from a questionable state by means
Of an exercise of extraordinary faculties simultaneously granted.

Really it's a wonder. I mean from your point of view, mainly.
As I myself see it, I merely play into your hands some tricks
You might choose to make use of to lend me a hand with my
Main task of recreating, or resurrecting, my human investment.
Let it not startle you that I speak to you plainly of such matters.

Then of course too, what you do to lift yourself out of an impasse,
Benefits not only you, because you do do it openly – otherwise
You turn into a dodo – and the result of that is extinction,
Which is what happens when illness is turned into a career.
You 'just love' the popular appeal your straying gains you.

*

So what am I saying: that when you have a headache, just draw
A pretty picture and you will be alright? Well, not exactly.
And why not? Because any creating you do has to begin
Within you, such as when you overcome some inclination to
Stray, to drift, to insist on self or to resist evil. In other words

Creation overcomes that which does not want to be created.
I certainly experience that myself every day when I present
My spirit to human beings. They do not welcome me with
Open arms, I can almost guarantee that. Nonetheless
I persist at times, and what pleasure it gives me to see

My work thrive. When humanity and divinity are creatively
Joined, then I make much of those who accept me.
I lead them into my sanctified garden here on earth
Where they may rest from their labours for a time – and
They have been labouring, that is true, in my absence.

How labour differs from work comes home to them then.
Looking back on their past they are liable to feel
Sorry for themselves but I soon put a stop to that
By introducing them to work of one sort or another.
At first I say to them: Look around! What do you see?

Often what happens then is that they praise what they see
And this is the most appropriate beginning for
Any kind of work, keeping in mind that work is creative.
Labour is necessary, work is creative, look at it that way.
I would regret if you made a thing out of either of these.

Just as you and I have stood on the peak and looked around
And you feasted your eyes on formidable prospects of
Glamorous distances, so does each one who begins to
Abide in me right away have much to praise, while
Not to do so implies a painful retrogression for him.

However this too, like all the pains that hinge upon
Creation and creativity, is soon enough understood
By the one whose soul cooperates with my intention,
So let there be no shilly-shallying in terms of causality,
Of blame and retribution, which is merely counterproductive.

You will say that I use a modern word here out of context,
So, to accommodate you, I will explain what I mean.
First of all, words are not modern or contemporary.
They are made, one or the other, by him who uses them,
Either disrespectfully of me or in honourable fashion.

Now I come to the matter in hand: Counterproductive
Is that which produces what is good by resisting it –
Which by no means implies that all that resists the good
Produces it. No, only what is counterproductive does.
I can see you are still not quite sure what I mean.

To help you a little further, I will speak of the difference
Between production and creation. This difference is
Remarkable. You will understand right away what I mean
When I say that a product is by no means a creation.
Creation is always good while production may be so.

This narrows down our search somewhat. Forgive me
For treating you like a child. Secretly I wish we could
Treat each other like children, however this is grammatically
Not quite right. Do you have the sense even now of
What I mean by good production? Not quite sure?

Well, I have found this before, that my personal examples
Are difficult to grasp. Good production leads you in a
Good direction, while bad production does the opposite.
Now, of course, I will have to explain what I mean by
A good direction. Let us take a few more careful steps

Down this mountain. Enough said? No? Still not quite?
Oh very well. In a good direction you approach and
Improve on your relation with the living god.
I sincerely hope you can make good sense of all this now.
There is such a thing as explaining a thing out of existence.

Soon your speech will bristle with things, and not a being
In sight. As we continue to descend this mountain
We do not neglect to feast our eyes on what surrounds us,
All of which is mysterious, marvellous and beautiful.
Who would want to become engrossed in explanation!

Returning to our incidental theme now, which is creation,
We may agree here, I hope, that during creation you and I
Cooperate in the most complete sense of that word.
We work side by side, like two friends who continue to
Help each other out gladly when the going gets tough.

*

Then suddenly, as never before, do you see that crevasse there,
It stretches the full width of the glacier and forms a barrier
To any man's progress, including yours and mine,
If no manner of way were to be found for us to bridge it.
You notice I speak differently, to give you an idea.

153

You should perhaps, before we go on, be informed that
Ideas are my angels and commonly I wish them entirely well;
To be fair, they are but agents of my well-wishing.
What I will not countenance, I tell you this right now, is
If your love for them diminishes your better love for me.

Indeed it would diminish you to do so, and since you are my
Main interest in this adventure which I call creation of humanity,
Take you on board now that angel-worship makes my blood boil,
Consequently yours run cold. If you must have ideas,
Immerse your ego in a vat of sweet wine first, to limber it.

Nonetheless yon glacier happens to be ideally placed
To allow you to come to grips with your ideal self,
Which is a self I would really prefer you to chop right off
As you would a diseased limb beyond healing, or an asset
That has long outlived its usefulness, so it drags you down.

Now how will you cross it when you get there, what with
That crevasse staring you in the face and making your legs
Quake? Very good. You think you might turn to me and
Ask me for a similar idea, only one that will serve us both to
Cross crevasses. I see you have by-passed your ideal self.

Then are you indeed no longer fond of being praised?
No longer willing to lend an ear to whisperings of flattery?
In fact are you willing to lay aside all preference of your own
Self in the presence of another self? Why then you may notice:
Any need to cross that crevasse has vanished into thin air.

And where that glacier poured itself, fat and irresponsible,
Down in front of us, angel choirs now sing your praises
For having turned to him they also praise, simultaneously;
And what a lesson is this, indeed, for a young man who,
If he would not have his heart broken, must break off his ego.

Not that I would expect anyone to do that voluntarily.
It has to be suggested in a roundabout way, such as
When love is first introduced as an ethical move and not
When those who don't know any better fall into it.
Let all parents teach their children how god is love.

May all parents show their children how this love works
When first the tragic representations of modern life
Make inroads on the young soul and instruct it in the various
Curfews that will eventually bottle it up altogether
Behind moral prohibitions and rampant sexuality.

No bridge exists from the modern cross to the contemporary
Stronghold. I call it the cross to which modern man is
Fastened and I call it a stronghold because contemporary
Men, women and children live safely in world without end.
Would it make sense for me to make allowances for those

Who reject me? Where would be the logic in that? Does the
Householder get together with the homemaker in order to
Invite, as guests, those whose entire reason for being is to
Reject and oppose house and home? Should the law of the land
Make allowances for those whose purpose is anarchy?

I consider the position of all who have truth in their sight.
Wherever I step into the world again and again I am slain.
The young pin their hopes on what has nowhere been realized.
The old have no wish to inform the young of the wasted life.
Disrespect, dishonour, despair, disease: these are manifest.

*

Let us descend to that plateau. To get to it we must traverse
That steep scree slope which, as you can see, drops down
Into nothing. You will wish to know what it signifies.
When we come to it you will understand. In the meantime
Place your feet carefully and avoid looking into the abyss.

There are those who would have you tread carefully but over
Splinters of glass and for no other reason, and these you must
Try to avoid. They fascinate and their task is to excite those
Who are addicted to sleep. Also you will come across those
Kind souls who have not yet discovered their strength.

Many others of an unfinished nature will cross your path
And each time you will try to help them find the piece of
Their nature that is missing, while the onus will be on you
To look away entirely from any negative state of things
So that I, who work within you, can make quick adjustments.

It is each time the critical spirit that would involve you in
Itself and in its machinations, to the point where you would
Begin to doubt your own credibility, which must not be.
The total alienation, of all that is modern, from me,
Works in your favour, in that, by avoiding it, you build strength.

So to that end you make a habit of withdrawing into yourself
For perfect rest, for the duration, while you admire, from a
Distance, the way I have laid out the good things of the earth,
Among them the silence of the woods, birdsong, sunshine and
Rain in measure, the changing seasons and variety of climate.

As you see we have arrived safely on the plateau from where
You may look into the past and into the future, to acquaint
Your eyes and ears, all your senses, which I call your new
Body, to the new reality that opens out to you a little more
Every day while you familiarize yourself with how you think.

Thought, as you will appreciate, is like a constant stream
And you may approach it, step into it, perhaps bathe, also
Divert yourself for the sheer pleasure of it, or learn how to
Set out on it to let it take you to distant lands from which you
Need never return because they are added to the here and now.

156

So you may understand that when you think, you immerse
Yourself in thought. Or else you may imagine thought as
That particular aspect of me from which you draw much
Sustenance of the sort that you need if you wish to glory
In your dependence on me and your freedom from me.

You are isolated from me at the moment because you have
Questioned your own worth and suitability. Too much thought?
No such thing. Only perhaps wrong or unsuitable thinking. –
From this rocky shelf, where we have disposed ourselves,
The visibility is exceptional. Allow the vision to come to you.

*

Even though the path down from the height should seem less
Arduous, nonetheless you are bound to cling to what you have
Achieved. You wish to own the peak, the credible performance.
At last the elements must bring you down. Storms, ice-cold,
Thunder and lightning, black clouds enshroud you. Be afraid.

Let gravity help you. Depend on your weight to indicate
How the next move might be made. I cannot do it for you.
We will not set our tent up and remain here forever. Learn
From the Gospels. I too trembled in view of the cross.
Now is the time for you to take advantage and not to tremble.

The belligerence of the popular voice angers and frightens you
When you look down, as soon as you contemplate giving in
To gravity even a little. How happy I am to be with you at this
Time. This is surely the trickiest trial of the new world, because
For once faith itself is tested. You are to depend upon it alone.

Know faith therefore as human being's resting-place. Believe
In me who has taken every step you are expected to take.
Believe also in me who is with you every step of the way.
Together we cannot go wrong. So what if a thousand eyes
Observe you and you feel obliged to behave as though you knew.

157

When faith turns into a faith, superstitiously, then I send
Reason, with its mask, to undermine that false security.
In the light of day they stripped one another of all decency.
What was I to do? I could not allow it. Eventually all hell
broke loose. The fires lit up the skies worldwide. I weep.

Come, let us take a few steps, we are far too cautious. Yes,
This is a kind of dizziness, of vertigo, you experience now.
Like all weaknesses, it makes room for strength, but you must
Believe that. Indeed this human-natural faculty of believing,
This tree trunk from the faith root, no longer does it stand.

In you I notice a readiness to believe logically and this I value.
Such foolishness, that reason and faith should ever have been
At loggerheads! But then faith was not faith, reason not reason.
An ideal situation had developed and I had to clamp down on it.
I will not allow the disciples of evil to destroy what I love.

You are once again at ease. The illusion of danger has passed.
Let circumspection guide you through that jumble of boulders
Up ahead. Be aware, some are moist and therefore slippery.
Your foot will glance off. A broken limb at this height is
No joke. Your poorly educated intellect rushes to conclusions.

Do not let it grieve you that I speak of your intellect like this.
Your sphere of interest will be truth, which is innate; however
Your intellect would be schooled in terms of it – and your will,
That which is commonly associated by the moderns with
Force and appetite, is subdued by compassion and humility.

While you lean on me you have nothing to fear, neither
Scarcity of substance nor superfluity of energy. Those are
The gifts of critical spirit, beyond all caution, as it, in turns,
Forces and seduces the confused passengers from one side
Of the ship to the other and back again, risking catastrophe.

Innate knowledge, by which I mean the knowledge that stems
From your perfected human nature, rises spontaneously to the
Surface for him whose hands are clean, so that here and now,
In the light of day, world-awareness brings it to contemporary
Fruition. I refer to this as the creative transformation process.

Do you see the cliffs down there below us? How will we
Get past them? Not until we come right up close to them
Will we be able to plan that part of the descent, so take
No precautions right now, you cannot in any case, but trust
That when the time comes, even from above we will find a way.

How to survive, that is the central issue for the young individual
Who feels the call to god from within, while he full well
Knows that innate knowledge is not arrived at for money.
There's no getting around it, this is the first test of his faith.
Does he believe he is more important to me than sparrows.

While he leans on good spirit he will have the real food
And shelter too will not be wanting. How can I expect him
To have the least notion of the real food, when the experts
Deal in Ersatz and call it the real thing? Make an allowance
For the lack of instinct. Encourage adolescent dreaming.

So much ignorance clogs up the well. Since the priests have
The least notion of all, really, and people still look up to them,
And teachers dabble in magic to make a name for themselves,
How will intimate human-natural knowledge be disseminated?
The search for external data I call extinct knowledge.

Whether the scientist searches among the masses of appearances
Or mostly he straps what he calls nature to the wheel,
A plethora of things rears up to his prying senses and
Offers him likely facsimiles which bear as much relation
To reality as a household cat to the teeth of a tiger.

159

Innate knowledge is of beings as they are, have been and will be
And you will learn how to approach them neither politely nor
Impolitely but with faithful courtesy, with the lightest of touches,
Respecting the willingness of each to reveal both its essence
And existence, for you to marry the two in the name of humanity.

Things are anxious beings that wish to come true. If you would
Kindly understand this and not give vent to sarcastic resentment
But at least wait for the truth to exercise a modicum of good
Will in your favour, there may be a chance for you, otherwise
Your number goes down to rock bottom and stays there.

Then you will come to the edge of those cliffs and turn away
In horror for your bare existence and you will return to the
Peak and stay there until your skin cracks, you limbs stiffen
And your bones turn brittle. I myself do not exist there and
In no way can I help you. They will say he was such a nice man.

They will wail and say: How could god let him perish, however
I did all I could. And never suppose that vengeance is mine.
Vengeance is always yours, from beginning to end, while for me
Mercy clings to every fibre of what chooses to be live, while
My being is merciful – however I can do nothing for the dead.

Idle curiosity tempts you to wonder what happens to the dead.
Why, simply look around. Some float to the top, others
Sink to the bottom, none of which has anything to do with me.
I am the god of the living and my heart goes out to them,
Which is to say I cooperate with them during their resurrection.
                                        *
Now it occurs to me that after all this strenuous thinking
A diversion might be in order. Rome was not built in one day
And your own resurrection is not to be viewed by you as
A stern discipline pursued with stoic rigour under
Spartan conditions. Never forget we are in this together.

160

One tragic reason why humanity has not evolved, even though
Development on many instances has come close to evolving,
Has always been that either individuals have left it in my hands
Or they independently strained to extend development
Beyond its human-natural boundaries, where demons roost.

We do wonder, in our various celestial spheres (bear with me)
Why our divinity is seen as so far beyond your capacities.
Some understood why the human element had to be thoroughly
Distinguished, so they learned to appreciate it in distinction.
I had set aside two-thousand years at the outset, which time is up.

Yes, the distinction of the human element – the first among you
Who understood what was needed rose to the occasion.
With bated breath we observed every move he made.
All depended in the end on whether he would strike the balance
Between man and god. When he made the break we cheered.

Now the stage was set, as you may appreciate. Do feel free
To recline on this slab of sandstone warmed by the sun.
Merely lend an ear to what I say; no need to participate.
So, as I say, the example was set, the reconstitution of humanity
Was now on its way and all that was needed was 'imitatio'.

However they would not take advantage of what he had made
Possible, that was the sad thing. Some, of course, did, to a point.
Also what he had made impossible, that too had to be understood.
I see on your face that look of puzzlement so familiar to me.
Think of it this way – and I will break this down into sections:
When someone has mended the leak, can it be mended again?

No, now is the time to fill that container. On the other hand,
If you do not believe that the container holds water, will you
Bother going to the well with it? Of course not. So there were
Those who practiced a foolish imitation and those who
Saw no reason to imitate nor anyone who might be imitated.

And yet each one who bears true fruit is available to do it
For all time. So help from within has been available for
Two millennia, though rarely addressed. The fact that you
Avail yourself of our help so assiduously while aiming
At your own perfection of being and doing is glorious.

*

I hope this has encouraged you. We are still some distance
From where the first stunted oaks cling to the barely
Corroded rock, however we will shortly arrive at a tarn
Where glacier water has collected and there you may
Slake your thirst and consider your fortunate position.

To be alive and then to have life, to be one of the living –
The beauty of that is underestimated by those who have
A strong constitution and they throw themselves into work,
But work of such an intensity that I feel I am sidelined,
And consequently, for lack of courage, they break down.

Courage, you see, is the one single element of your human
Nature that essentially depends more on me than on you.
When you lack courage, you lack me. Then, of course,
Bravado is not courage, so once again you do well to
Look into your heart to check whether your god is present.

Also, lack of courage is not yet necessarily cowardice,
It is merely the indicative stage that precedes it. So the
Questions is, how can you test yourself. Surely you would
Wish to be ready for every eventuality. Why wait until
Cowardice sets in and you find yourself bound, in a sack?

If the finite world has moved in where I wish to be and
You cannot for the world come up with the solution to a
Single problem, emotional, psychic or carnal, then you
Dither, or you hasten and rush, anxious for an end
Or panic for the lack of an end, and I cannot help you.

We are bound in merciful love from birth, and in wisdom,
And beyond the shadow of a doubt we set out upon the earth
As a single being in twofold manner, human and divine.
Why, you might very well ask, are you endowed with this
Ability to reflect upon yourself both within and without?

Simply for the reason that you are created the stewards
Of all creation. To that end is your power always renewed,
But as soon as you impress yourself upon creation, to bend it
To your means and ends, the mighty one asserts himself,
Supposedly in your interest; you mistake might for power.

It takes courage to come to terms with the mighty one, then
To destroy him. Destroy by removing the structure. This is
Not child's play, neither will the mighty one help you to
Destroy himself, that should go without saying, however
Often I wonder why it takes so long to arrive at that insight.

This also demonstrates the importance of courage in life,
That you should be given this mighty one to cope with,
To recognize and overcome him, that the child might grow
Into manhood and set out upon his task as steward of
All he surveys, not as a meddler in things but powerfully.

And by power – I will never tire of saying this – I mean
Ability to do good, to use your talents and genius in the
Interest of the heavenly mandate, the kingdom of heaven,
Or however you like to imagine it, and in line with
The one who first showed the true way, and shows it now.

Why should it matter to you whether I speak to you as
Father or son, in spirit or in the flesh, once I have immersed
My being in all that is, my will in all that is done, my
Essence in all that exists? Why should anyone doubt that
Humanity touches me deeply and defines 'my nature'?

Once you search within yourself for the definition of what it
Means to do good, you are bound to arrive at the knowledge of
My nature, my birth, while simultaneously you are confronted
By the mighty one who insists he is spirit 'untainted' by
What he calls sinful human nature in need of baptismal blessing.

Well, there you have it, it's make-your-mind-up time now.
Take courage, with me on board, and steer a course for
Evolution and resurrection – or follow the dictates of the
Mighty one who teaches sacrifice not mercy, who calls himself
Powerful and does no good, who is critical modern spirit.

Ask yourself, why not: How shall I bind the mighty one?
Time and again I am left to my own devices and I discover
How soon I fly into a rage, how I force, assuming for benefit,
Others and my circumstances; I make demands and utter threats.
I insist that what I have in mind is the only right way.

This is how the mighty one behaves. He leaves you with no
Courage in your heart, only shame for being ignored and
Guilt after ignoring others. He scratches out your eyes
So that you suppose you see more clearly and he breaks your
Bones to make you fit into cramped quarters, to please him.

Explain to yourself that courage is not the same as ruthless
Behaviour. You insist you are free as a bird because you are
Devoid of care for others, especially for those closest to you.
The mighty one sacrifices you to his obscene appetites
And 'calls you out', so that you will fight with him.

How will you know that you have no courage? I mean
Even before need for courage emerges? Look into a mirror
And imagine you are someone else. Suddenly you will wish
You had spoken to that stranger in a kindlier fashion –
That you had loved husband or wife instead of being right.

Finally learn to pray, because during prayer I step right up
Close to you. During prayer the mighty one has no
hold over you. He loses interest in you. It takes courage to pray.
Shall I teach you how to pray? Wish to pray and I will
Stand or walk beside you. Now we pray as one human being.

You are walking a little too fast. Please slow down
So that you can hear what I am saying. This is a path
Tramped into the scree by goats. The son of man
Desires to make your acquaintance. I can see that you
Cannot imagine whom I mean. I will find a better name.

The son of man is the one who lets you know suddenly
That the time is ripe. This, however, is the expression of a
particular culture, so it has to be translated to fit in with
your particular culture, otherwise how can you make
sense of it. Will you perhaps, one day, be such a translator?

I shall give you an example. Empty your mind of all
Thoughts and images and hear what I have to say to you.
If the son of man did not appear when the time is ripe,
He would do so when you are most vulnerable. Now can you
Imagine how all your plans and expectations would crumble?

Try to understand that I know the time and you do not.
Therefore I must try to let you know the time. Now, for example,
Is the time for you to linger over what you have heard me say.
I can see, by the fact that you had begun to linger, that you had
Listened to what I was saying and that you heard what I meant.

You would, of course, be smart to learn how to recognize
the time when the son of man is about to appear and then to
make a good habit of that. He always brings the best of news,
if you but knew that. And you are right away involved,
either in the catastrophe, if you were not ready, or beneficially.

165

Of course there are small and large breakdowns. Always pray.
Readiness is all. Do not allow yourself to drift off into
Clouds of self-satisfaction or, conversely, to get carried away
By the immensities of your many sensations. The son of man
Is the growth-factor par excellence. Now is always the time.

The time for your resurrection, as you may recall, was truly
The crucial time as such, and so it is for all those who
Arrive at that moment, are ready for it, and know what to do.
I only wish I could tell each one of my chosen ones exactly
How to prepare, however the individual contribution is needed.

*

Even now, although we are still high above the tree-line,
Some of the elements are making their peculiar characteristics
Felt. At this moment the sun lets you know it is time to adjust
To the mid-day heat. Its rays counsel adaptation and its light,
As sunlight, coaxes to the fore acknowledgment of world.

Know therefore that world is endless. Infinite the elements,
Choose them for your creative process before they overly
Press you, for world is my gift to man, challenge to mankind.
Those who evolve like you make world more accessible.
Think of it now as essentially and originally sacramental.

Do you not perceive even now – better, do you not behold –
The wonder of world, prior to its falsification, imminent
To intuition? Be exceedingly glad; I mean beyond any
Cause for gladness, except that gladness is the cause
As supplied by you, to exist for the sacramental advantage.

Knowledge gradually accumulates, as your body of knowledge.
On it you depend when you wish to teach, to inform, also to
Communicate beyond the status quo, when you experiment
So as to be able to add to the knowledge sought by others:
Knowledge sacramental, knowledge elemental, both good.

Never lie down under pain. I have lengthened the time available
For learning how to suffer intelligently and creatively so that
Whatever comes your way you will know how to turn it into
Ethical quantity of one sort or another, for others to ingest,
To imbibe. Keep in mind that only god *is* good, but you *do* it.

World is a blessing, is one blessing after the other, for that is
My intention, so that you may thrive as a whole human being
In community. Part of your task, and an important part, is
That you know world as my original intention, and you will
Succeed in this inasmuch as you communicate my intention.

You live on earth in world; be aware of the difference.
Earth is material and particular, so that you may create,
Even as I do, on a daily basis, all that is required to make
A home, first for yourself, and then for all things that exist
As yet in limbo, as if deserted by their original creator.

None of this will you achieve unless you accept that
Man has spoiled my creation, mostly through disobedience,
But then by outright rejection of myself in person.
You yourself are a man and therefore you bear this burden
Of guilt and responsibility for all that you experience as faulty.

If I myself in person had not come to your attention
In a way that cannot be taught by rote intellectually,
Neither would your responsibility have occurred to you
And neither would you have been able to assist me now
With the total renewal of what is meant by heaven and earth.

For two millennia this process of renewal has been on the cards
And many have done their best to push the work forward,
Either by following my lead, one culmination after the other,
Or by waiting for me to show them the next step towards the goal
And so the work has proceeded, by both direction and attraction.

First renewal of heaven, renewal of earth, each separately,
That is how the process is well understood, since the mass
Of ancient knowledge as such is not open to comprehension.
So that has been the work for two millennia, instigated
By me in person, against a backdrop of despair and confusion.

Rightly this work may be described as developmental
and it has proceeded on both sides of the divide.
If you had looked from here onto what you see now,
Your vision would have been double, sensible and conceptual,
and always you would have come down on one side or the other.

Clearly neither old sense plus new concept nor new sense
Plus old concept, like old patch on new garment or new wine
In old vat, could succeed. However all such premature attempts
Also presaged the fullness of time to come, when heaven
And earth, both renewed, should unite and be joined and

This will be your task as soon as we arrive at the base of
The mountain we have climbed, from which we descend now.
You, inasmuch as you evolve, succeeding your development,
Will show the so-called kingdom of heaven as the marriage
Of heaven and earth, itself evolving, all being as one.

*

If life ever gets too serious for you, once you have commenced
Upon the shocking foxtrot of everyday existence – which is
Not to be circumvented, please don't try – then cast yourself as a
comic actor in a play of your own contemporary invention. This
Shall run parallel with your eternal live within and without you.

Yes, I take it that this is an altogether novel notion for you,
Brought up as you were by bone-dry sycophants and lesbian
Dames of the realm, excuse me, surely you know what I mean.
I mean that your eternal life should have an everyday existence
Merrily running parallel, the one not knowing what the other does.

168

Of course there is cross-fertilization, that goes without saying.
The work we do mostly goes on in secret. You refer to me
And I to you. For example the fact that you will be
Following me, even persistently at times, need never alert or
Alarm the butcher or the chap you meet when out for a walk.

They however are among the direct beneficiaries of our work
And very likely they will not know it. Is that not remarkable?
I say they are among them. There will also be those who sit
Grim-faced at the bus stop, laden with grief, ready to kill
The next person who seems to question their right to exist.

Oh I know, how are you supposed to distinguish between the
Shysters who will never have a true bone in their body and
My little ones who sadly have some of the worst hang-ups.
All I can say at the moment is: When the time comes,
Look quickly in my direction and receive the crucial hint.

As for our parallel, everyday existence, don't overdo it.
No need to be polite but don't be impolite. Oh let's face it
You won't be able to be polite in any case, however
You may be tempted and then I shall have to trip you up –
Sorry, I cannot actually allow you to adopt social graces.

I have more to say about this. Don't play the fool. That is,
If you find yourself funny you are out on a limb cutting it off.
You are merely wanting to be liked. Stop it immediately!
I mean it. Persist and you will regret it. Take my word for it.
Both wanting to be liked and wanting to be loved are taboo.

Why is this so? Because you will be too busy liking and loving.
If it were not for our everyday existence – which you, by the way,
Will shape entirely as you see fit – your work would lose all
Perspective, do you know what I mean? You would, for example,
Imagine that you have to invent pain for yourself, or temptation.

There have always been those – I hate even to think of it –
Who felt 'the call', as they like to call it, and what is the
First thing they do? They separate themselves off from normal,
Everyday existence – you know, out here 'where it's at' –
By putting on a dog collar, by entering a monastery and

Staying there for the rest of their lives, or by moving into
A cave, for goodness' sake, and then, of course, things get
Boring; all the useful, practical troubles and problems are
Siphoned off artificially and the next thing that happens is
They abuse children, they self-harm; there was even one
Who prayed fervently for a sickness – in her germ-free cell.

That is so gruesome! I do not like to do it but I spit them out.
That is why I say to you: When the time comes, at the foot
Of the mountain, be an individual person 'out here'. Yes,
Out here! Know what this means, to exist out here, I mean
Especially when you live eternally. That goes on happily
While you trust me to place you and move you wherever I like.

I noticed how you looked at me there as if I were caught up
In some contradiction. God forgive you. I forgive you.
Did I not mention cross-fertilization earlier? Yes I did.
In other words, just as your everyday existence feeds your
Eternal life, so does your eternal life flow into your existence.

So do not be overly surprised if suddenly you make a move
That does not exactly fit snugly into your social environment.
Do not do it on purpose. If it happens, fine. Take it from there.
You will find that I am perfectly able to pull you out of the soup.
I will put words in our mouth the wisdom of which will

Astonish you. So play along. You are not two people with
Mutually unpredictable issues that need to be sorted, no,
You are amphibian, equally at home with people and with
Human beings – with those who know me and those who do not.
All the same, avoid those who proactively reject me.

Here is a secret now. When you yourself are rejected because –
Well, because of me, then here is your golden opportunity.
Suffer the consequences and evolve a bit more. In other words,
Bear fruit. Get to work. Down in the dumps? Get to work!
Up in seventh heaven because something has worked out for you?

Now you are on dangerous ground. Quietly withdraw, restrain and
Subdue yourself, overcome your ego – in other words: create!
Actually all your work will be creative – mind that slippery
Ledge, this is a dangerous traverse. Even the goats avoid it.
Speaking of which, the goats have their work cut out for them.

You, by comparison, cut out your own work. Do not wait for
Me to tell you what to do. I don't need servants or slaves.
Those who insist on being slaves lead a sorrowful existence.
I'm sorry, but I cannot take to them. However I do not reject them.
There you go, that is an important insight for you.

*

You will wonder now about the weakness that is setting in
after that cheerful sprint down-slope in the blistering sun.
Why not look forward to the time when we approach our
Goal, when you will take all the reins in your capable hands
And no more looking back to the time of your development.

I will always be with you in the guise of someone who
Has your best interests at heart, who straightens the path,
Who guides your every step as you take upon yourself
The sorrows and grief of our friends and turn them into
Compassionate acts. That is the work I intend for you.

At the present moment your step is not secure, so by all means
Lean on me as we proceed along the rest of our downhill
Journey. There is no point in wildly leaping ahead when
The joy brought on by youth and fresh air energizes you.
Try to be mindful at all times of energy as raw material.

171

Right now you have next to no energy, so you might as well
Learn how to draw on strength that lies readily available for
Each and every human being at all times. While you mistake
Energy, which has the 'feel' of strength, for strength itself,
You cannot be entrusted with strength, with physical power.

It is unidentifiable by the senses, think of that for the moment.
A feeling is a rock against which you are liable to stub your foot.
A thought is the flight of a bird – not suitable for your own flight.
Let power, the ability to do good, be your human identity
And know that power is not might, political and arbitrary.

Make no effort to memorize these words. The mere fact that
It is I who speaks them to you guarantees, if you hear me,
That when the time comes for you to employ this wisdom,
You will find it ready to hand, in one way or another and
No need to recall the word when the deed will realize it.

Power is the power of god and I keep it for myself and for
Those who are learning – and have learned – the wisdom of
The life that arrives on doves' feet, utterly unidentifiable
In itself. There is strength in my weakness and you may
Readily identify it, however there is no death in this life.

If you must know – and you are sure to question me later –
Dying, in your case, and equally in the case of those like you,
Is merely another word for loss of power. You will in future
Understand the death that is my death more readily if you
Think of it as limitation and guideline, as liberty in freedom.

Those who, like you, would realize my power world-wide,
May enjoy my companionship in each and every walk of their
Existence on earth, whether they build or tear down, construct
Or shape, all with the intention, unavoidably, to demonstrate
My love as good will, my good will as love, my care as joy.

*

I would have you know what powerful being is. Any exercise
of whatever faculties you possess at the time, be it in dream,
in fantasy, in logic or rational awareness, has me as its centre.
Therefore why would you ever look elsewhere when the
time comes to express yourself, to say what only you can say?

I say look to me for the being that substantiates your own being.
Then, if it happens that at night you cannot sleep, do not ask
why not and curse your fate but simply lean on me so that
what little strength of myself you can bear will come to you
and then you perform to your heart's content, even at night.

Fate is in fact inconsequential, a nonentity for which you pay
dearly if ever you stoop so low as to take up with it. I suggest
you identify, as soon as possible, the various characteristics
of this drain on good sense, this overture to mortal misery.
Learn what it means to ease yourself into my immortal being.

And yes, the emphasis is on ease, not on force or industry.
The lion's share of all the action and passion you can crowd
into a moment rests within you as my being, not as your effort.
What you must do: – Ask yourself are you driven to it and
Could you possibly refrain if your human being depended on it?

I choose to remind you at this moment of your human being
Precisely because fate as destiny, this twin impostor,
Would play such a role when the modern spirit would impose,
For one thing, its 'need for happiness'. If this spirit is unhappy
Let that mean to you that you yourself are content within me.

The search for happiness, for a meaningful life, for some worthy
Identity, this is not to draw your attention to itself but entirely
To me within you, where I, as the being I am, search out
The one who you are in yourself, bright and shiny like a new
Penny longing to be spent in the interest of others like you.

*

173

Look now within yourself, to see what you can see. Do the
Visions and the dreams that will eventually disturb you
Begin to lay down traces of themselves? Stand still now
And consider what I say. Fellow mortals, at this point,
Draw breath and feel fortunate not to feel implicated.

You may leave them to their feelings. Yes, close your eyes
And consider what it is that comes your way. Your body
Is no longer attached to your flesh. Forget all theories of
Body and soul, together or apart, also top of the range
Survival theories. The modern religions cannot help you.

I am about to implant in you the new understanding.
Fervour, vitality, the talent for being live, all these intertwine
To produce a new outlook on world environment. Your body
Is now invisible. Your flesh – which is what you and others
Look at – opens the door to many new carnal possibilities.

You are now in the possession of your new body. These eyes,
Upon which I lay my spirit finger, will now be capable of
Sight both within and without, and to such a degree that
Your new body incorporates cheerfully all that you truly
See, without hindrance from the world wanted and wished.

A time will come when you will long for joy and it will
Not be forthcoming and you will blame yourself for being
Remiss, for having failed, and you will search among the
Thousand things, the deluge of unwanted sensations, for
The life to which you have become accustomed.

Sadness will pursue you through the night and you will
Wonder why you cannot find me, however I will be
As close to you as I am now and busy on your behalf.
So learn to interpret the hard times in terms of the
Good times. Perhaps you have been misled to expect

The sensation of life as its guarantee. Your resurrection
Was never intended to be other than the life of evolution,
When a man learns to live and shows others how to do it.
It is also the time when time often stands still and your
Casual existence lends itself to many interpretations.

The food you require from me is available when you ask.
You buckle down to the task of asking, because this is
Quite often a technical achievement. There is a right
Time for it, the time of scarcity and dearth, not when
Nourishment occurs to you as a mere possibility.

So identify the time of need, which is also the time of
Plenty for him who understands. Your flesh is not
Designated for the grave but my spirit delights in it.
Do I not daily create that which most likely will
Grind to a halt for the lack of human cooperation?

Here we have arrived at this dried up stream bed
Where once upon a time a glacier's melt-water
Washed these boulders that now lie exposed
To the sun during the day and the freezing cold at night
So that soon they will crack. Seek your images within.

All that exists upon earth awaits your arrival and also
The arrival of others like you who have made the break.
Not only those who do great things will survive but
Those whose survival abuts eternal life and they
Step across and manage the connection to my planning.

*

We are going to continue for a time in this stream bed
even though the going is tough. However the weather
is in our favour, by which I mean that we are not
inconvenienced by it as we descend to sea level while I
instruct you in ways that convenience you to the truth.

If I did not exist on earth within those who abide by my
Instruction, there would be no truth to speak of, because
The world of things would be a jumble, impenetrable to
Minds whose sole existence amounted to the tactics
Required for 'living from hand to mouth', birth to death.

Since the time when I entered the world, my own creation,
The truth – by which I mean, at the present moment, the way
Creations and creatures all fit together – since that time,
As anyone with a bit of sense would expect, the truth may be
At least guessed at, however also known and understood.

Well you may guess why it should be an advantage
For anyone to know the truth, in other words, why it should
Matter to human beings that they are in truth human beings
And therefore not merely beings like all other beings. Why
Should they wish to enjoy this special status and be glad of it?

The answer to this is the old story: That is how I
Created them. Those who accuse me of doing a poor job –
And there *are* those, as you know – they overlook this
Small detail, namely that I created them with a variety
Of abilities, and among these is the ability to believe.

I created them with faith and the ability to believe. So you ask:
Why, then, do so many have no faith and no ability to believe?
This has to do with what it means to create – to be a creator.
Whatever we create, we can only create it in our image
And the truth is that I too am able to believe or not to believe.

I tell you this in all confidence, so that you will keep it
Tightly locked in your heart and not waste it on those whose
Created abilities have deteriorated to the point where they can
No longer imagine anything greater than themselves, which is
The beginning of the road of deterioration towards extinction.

So since I believe as I choose, at liberty to discern between
What is worth believing and what is not, that is also how
All my creatures, including human beings, are equipped,
At liberty to believe what they like. Those who assume
That human beings should at least be able to boast of an

Inborn certainty, well, let's put it this way, they like to boast.
No, certainty is either acquired in particular fashion
Or else it depends upon a sufficiency of faith and belief.
I believe that you are able to understand what I am saying
And for that good reason I continue with my instruction.

So the faith I have I pass on to human beings to a sufficiency,
Depending, of course, on the material that is available to me.
People multiply and that is their god-given right.
Among them my creation flowers, and at times to great beauty,
however resurrected humanity is a matter of fruition.

So if you feel you must concern yourself with this particular
'question', as I call it, you may imagine, for but one example,
That popularity exists in the service of humanity, always
To the fullest possible extent of its respective talent.
Humanity is the essence of being and human beings exemplify it.

In a sense, if you ever find yourself thinking in reverse,
Which is not an entirely unenjoyable pastime, you also have to
Think a beginning for everything, including yourself,
And so these many interesting and edifying creation stories
'come into being' – I dare say you appreciate my choice of words.

I advise no one to make a career of thinking in reverse.
Eventually imagination cries: 'Let me out of here!'
Then, in its absence, the strangest theories and sons of theories
Step on stage: 'the survival of the fittest' and 'black holes'.
Popularity now no longer aids but deserts humanity.

In that case I avert my gaze and then look the other way,
In the direction of forward thinking again, my default setting.
In truth there is no beginning and no end. They speak of
The birth of God, and I don't like to interfere, but let's face it,
The 'nature of god' is often a 'misappropriation of funds'.

After all, I have created all beings and continue to create them
But spirit does not create itself. Thinking in reverse can cause
Many difficulties for people and they would do well to pay
More respect to what human beings come up with in terms of
The truth of matter, which would allow them to smile more.

Matter, you see, inasmuch as it pertains to the created earth,
Invites all right-thinking people to fulsome appreciation,
So that they will learn the measure of their developed minds.
– Please be careful. What you are doing is 'boulder hopping'.
Those boulders are wet and slippery, as you noticed.

Yes, matter. A complicated topic, if I say so myself.
You can infinitely divide it, there's no end to that either,
However it's knowing when to stop. You may not come across
Any difficulty yourself in that direction, however you will wish
To inform and guide those who mistake matter for substance.

Materialist notions are always a 'bind'. Along comes the sad
Reaction of the spiritualist, who doesn't know where to begin.
Avoid those unfortunate extremes by fully understanding
What I mean by *substance*, namely that which underlies
All that is or desires to be, its essence, which is humanity.

You look at me, your eyes two pools of consternation
And I fully understand your difficulty. Why do you suppose
You are able to exercise this capacity (unique to human beings)
To understand all beings? I will tell you. Now look at me again
And listen closely: Because all that is is essentially human.

Does that or does that not make you right away wonder
How humanity might be imagined? How it might be conceived?
What else could be said about it other than that it is the essence
Of being? – I am sorry to have to disappoint you. That which is,
Is human and there the matter ends. There are implications.

Matter, for example. Once you understand humanity as substance
You will no longer be tempted to make a thing out of matter,
Which is another way of saying: you will not get carried away
With the production of endless amounts of this and that
Merely to satisfy that perfectly legitimate appetite for substance.

This is the shakiest of the unstable modern structural principles,
That scarcity of substance is anxiously misperceived as a thing
That can be cured by producing seemingly endless amounts
Of material commodities. Terrestrial resources must therefore
Also appear to become scarce, to encourage research for substance.

Oh if only I could impress upon you the meaning of 'scarcity of
Substance'! Why does it seem to be scarce? Only because you have
Not yet begun to lean on me sufficiently in order to take due
Advantage of humanity that originates with me – or else because
You have grown lax in your behaviour, and I no longer count.

Yes, your humanity is to increase; you are to become more human.
And this is where I will explain to you now your innate relation
To all other beings. You relate to them in a way in which they
Cannot relate to one another. This is due to your ability
To understand, which you share only with other human beings.

Sooner or later you will wish to accumulate substance. Once you
Understand the importance of this and you learn to interpret those
Borderline sensations when substance 'should' be accumulated,
You will also come to the conclusion that you have innately
Within you – or perhaps I should say as part of your make-up –

that which identifies and characterizes all other beings. Now
How can anyone be expected to imagine this! What, for example,
Is the identity and character of a plant? Ah well, you see, that is
Precisely the purpose of the interest you take in plants. There is
An attraction and now you set out to capitalize on that.

So due to the interest you take in a being in the light of the fact
That somehow you will be able to identify its characteristics
In common with some of your own, to that extent and degree you
Add on to your substance, your humanity. Also now imagine
What good it will do that being? Will it not confirm it in its being?

You see all around you nowadays, the increased interest taken
In the living environment of the earth by many who understand.
At the same time thousands upon thousands spoil the earth's face,
Taking no thought of how, as a consequence, their humanity is
Gradually depleted, for the lack of empathetic understanding.

More important than the earth are the human beings living on it.
Therefore you must concentrate on educating those who hold
The reins in ignorant hands, that they will respect those who,
Unlike themselves, understand. Only the truth can overcome
Ignorance and in the absence of love even truth must fail.

Modern science is extinct. It does not further human substance
But misreads all substance-scarcity and concentrates on supply
Of matter serviceable and matter sympathetic, which only
Eats into itself while the seeming scarcity is not recognized.
Now I will tell you how to recognize seeming substance scarcity.

When panic sets in, know that the time has come for under-
standing a consanguinity with another being or other beings.
When you feel panic, right away set yourself the task of
Looking within yourself for that relationship with the one
You fear, the one you hate, the one you disrespect or loathe.

First you should look to the human being. I say 'should' because
Invariably some guilt or shame is involved which you must
Overcome. I say 'must' because some necessity plays a role.
Also I say 'overcome', for which you may come up with
Merciful love. And I say 'may' because this love is ever available.

Panic is akin to anxiety. Suddenly everything is wrong and
On top of you. Think about this in detail ahead of time. Practice
Dealing with panic, so that you will be a little ready when the
Time comes. Panic is not really a feeling but an existential
Emergency, which can leave you helpless, discouraged and mad.

Learn, when you come across madness in others, they have
Not yet overcome the guilt or shame brought on by panic.
How can you help them understand? Simply by doing the understanding for them, even in their presence. Panic also means
lethargy, horror, illness – incurable until panic is overcome.

So panic is the sign of seeming scarcity of substance. Panic is to
Bring you around from matter-worship to humanity-love. Panic,
In all its forms and guises, may therefore be welcomed by him
Who understands, on behalf of him who does not yet understand.
Among those who do not understand, panic spreads like a forest fire.

True understanding is compassionate. Consider also, again, that
Not only human beings are to be understood but all beings.
Science should be knowledge for understanding, however
Modernity has coined its own language and the emphasis is on you
To overcome this barrier. You must interpret compassionately.

While I speak with you like this I am able to look forward
To the time when all human science will be compassionate,
Not materialistic. In the meantime flames must continue to
Burn up the dross. Poisons will continue to contaminate and
So-called natural disasters must bring populations to their senses.

*

I cannot guide you through every nook and cranny of your
Existential memory. Much of what you draw on from
Past experience exists, as it were, under your permanent
jurisdiction and you may dwell on it or disregard it.
This is up to you, however consider the consequences.

As a mature human being, you are sometimes bound to be
In your stride and not to be interrupted by angels or demons.
You are also bound to make mistakes, from which you will
Learn, much like a child, intuitively and instinctively,
So never fear the step into the dark and the slip across ice. –

When we arrive at the foot of this mountain you will no longer
See me as you see me now, however you will see me
'In the round' so to speak, which is, of course, a step
In the right direction, also an improvement, inasmuch as you will
No longer be limited by judgment and progress in space and time.

People made themselves responsible for a tremendous error
When, at the end of my time on earth as human personality,
I assured them they would see me again and they misunderstood.
They expected to see me again with their unresurrected eyes.
This, of course, is impossible and a good thing too.

You yourself, I hope, are perfectly in the clear now about
What I mean when I say that you see me now and after we part
You will see me again. Yes, there will be a gain. That is quite
Correct and to be kept in mind, especially when a loved one
Departs from the earth. Grief is to teach you to see him again.

When I was on the earth, as I say, in human personality,
I was eager to draw attention both to myself and to the beauty
Of faith. When those who refused to understand then turned
Faith into a faith, soon there were many faiths, especially
The faith of those whom I think of as permanent outsiders.

The task of these outsiders, who prefer to remain enslaved,
Is to operate from a direction quite opposite to that of those
Who insist on remaining ancient, and I cannot blame them;
However, as you believe, so you proceed or recede.
It is not the task of merciful spirit to judge those who refuse it.

It is always a great pleasure to see me and those to whom it is
Given to see me (there will always be enough of them to go
Around) will tell the others what they see, each in his own way,
And this will be a pleasure for them then. I do not hide myself.
Of course there will be times when you seek to see me but cannot.

Why, in any case, would you wish to see me? I ask, because
There are those who become downright addicted to seeing god
And they neglect the work that should arise out of their vision.
These are the mystics for whom I am nothing but an exercise in
Piety and my heart goes out to them but does them no good.

I must just say a few words, not about the mystic vision, which is
Good, but about mysticism, which cannot brook the least contradiction because it is, so to speak, wrapped up in itself and in its
contemplation of itself. Narcissus was, in that sense, the first
mystic and you know how he ended. I insist that you stay clear.

I have to warn you that much that came easy to you until now
Will for a while cause you all sorts of difficulties, which bring
Your resurrection, as the ongoing physical procedure that it is,
To your attention. Think one step at a time. After all you have
Acquired many bad habits of wilful, forceful accomplishment.

I teach you especially the singular virtue of exceeding gladness
As the key to transition. When the going gets tough, be exceedingly
Glad, if you can imagine. Your muscular will has a bone to pick
With you every time you apply your concerted faculties.
Body and soul, flesh and spirit, all contribute now to your physical

183

action and passion rolled into one and no longer compartmental.
Again and again be more glad than troubled. Whatever faculty
You specialized while you developed and it became egotistic,
Now it insists on its rights, wishes to be employed at any cost.
Learn to be exceedingly glad and make a good habit of that.

What the trouble really amounts to shall be of no interest to you.
You are far too busy joining me as a whole person, carefully
Diligent, sweetly cooperative and longing to be helpful,
Just as I long to be able to assist you in ever way possible.
Be here and not there. This is the default position for resurrection.

Here and now, that is the point on the graph for the value of
x and y. You return to this point and you leave from it. Those
who actively contradict every move you make will be answered
by me, not by you. You have to be disciplined, are you not glad?
I mean are you not glad that what you yourself cannot do, I do?

Also be proud of the fact that much that I cannot do for you
You yourself will be doing. How could anything please us and
Satisfy us more than that we assist one another, human beings
And their god in unison, making eternal life on earth not only
Possible but actual. It is for this that we both create, in unison.

*

Think only of what you wish to achieve. Then accept all the
Help you can get. There is no experience without pain, only
Pain that is suffered and pain that is rejected. While you
Think of me as merely an illusion, at your beck and call,
This prevents me from doing my best for you, so take advice.

When they give you advice, consider it carefully. There are
Those who have no notion of what you are about and they
Blab the first thing that comes into their head; it makes them
Feel better. Then there are those with a lively appreciation
Of what it means to stand in line for my favours for a time.

184

I cannot secure you against pain. However I can assure you that
Your pain is always and every time a sign of progress and
While you accept it as such it works in your favour. There is
So much that needs to be resurrected and so few willing to do it
That you may count yourself blessed for being able to understand.

Understanding, as you know, implies an exchange of substance,
So that the being you properly understand enters into a type of
Marriage with you. How good this is might not occur to you at
That precise moment but not to worry. Pain means progress.
How you behave under diverse circumstances counts.

We are now at the end of this particular journey together and
I can see that you are having a difficult time. You are afraid that
Afterwards you will be 'lost for words'. Please, no need to worry.
The next word is even now standing ready for you to make its
Acquaintance. We have come full circle. Take time for rest.

* * * * *

www.ingramcontent.com/pod-product-compliance
Lightning Source LLC
Chambersburg PA
CBHW060504290526
45791CB00001B/264